Blindsided by the Walking Dead

"From surviving the streets to slaying the geeks"

IronE Singleton

With Juliette Terzieff

ISBN: 978-0-9890210-1-2

Blindsided by the Walking Dead

Myriad Press

Cover design: newNsight Design & Photography
Author Photographers:
Derek Blanks (front cover) & Commaleta Singleton (back cover)

Contents

In loving memory of my mother Catherine Singleton
and all the others that left us too soon.
You will always be remembered...

Chapter 1
The Prayer

The creak of hinges tore my attention away from the day's homework. I turned to see Uncle Larry filling up the doorframe to our bedroom like a loaf of bread filling up a pan as it bakes. I noted right away he had one hand on the doorknob, the other on his hip, and a crease spreading across his wide brow. He was built like a mike—an inside linebacker in layman's terms. He'd even played a bit in his younger days. Right now he looked as if he were primed for a snap to unleash some serious hurt on the opposing team's quarterback.

"Sonny boy, you need to come wit'me for a few," he said quietly and turned to walk down the narrow hallway toward his bedroom.

As I laid down my pencil, I wondered what infraction I might be called out for. Uncle Larry had a quiet way about him; he rarely raised his voice when speaking. When his voice dropped to a whisper it was almost as bad—and sometimes worse—than when he started screaming. Anytime we found ourselves leaning in to hear Uncle Larry speak, we knew something serious was about to go down.

I paused on my way out the door to shut off the light before following in his footsteps. We hadn't been living with Momzie and Grandpa Ray very long by then, and while I knew the rules of the apartment, sometimes I just forgot. How many rules could a nine-year-old be realistically expected to remember? Grandpa Ray's work was the kind that made a man feel ancient at only fifty years old. Manual labor at a tech steel manufacturing plant left him with little energy for more than sleeping when the workday was done. Larry became the enforcer. If I was already in trouble, I didn't want to make it worse by adding to the power charges. The family was already struggling to pay all the bills. Every penny counted in those days. Every. Single. Penny.

Uncle Larry's room was on the second floor along with two other bedrooms and a bathroom. The biggest belonged to Grandma Ethelrine and Grandpa Ray. The apartment was their home, so it was only right they had the best room. Uncle Larry—who most people call Big Larry on account of his son, Larry Jr.—had the second bedroom to himself. My older brother Tracy, our momma Catherine, and I shared the third room. Cat wasn't around much. I missed her when she was gone, but it simplified the sleeping arrangements. Big Larry and Momzie—Miss Rine as the neighborhood knew her—took care of us. She nurtured, giving us hugs and emotional support; he taught. I wasn't quite sure what kind of lesson I was about to receive, though.

"Come sit next to me, Robby. Close that do' on yo way in." Larry beckoned me into the room. I obeyed without question. Larry sat and removed his shoes and socks and placed them near his nightstand, even though it was hours before dinner time. It didn't make much sense to me. Why was Uncle Larry sitting there without footwear? What had I done now?

"Life ain't always pretty, sonny boy, but every day is a gift. I want you to remember that," he said. I sat down next to him on the bed. "You weren't put here on this Earth to get what you want, any way ya wan' it, the quickest way you can. Ya hear me? You here, because God placed you on this Earth for a purpose. It is His will." He paused and looked me in the eye. I knew he was gauging whether I understood we were having a real bona fide man-to-man conversation, though I was years away from the age when I needed to shave like a real man.

He held my gaze for several seconds and nodded.

"Okay now, take those off and place 'em next to mine," he instructed, pointing to my shoes, "I got something I want to share wit' you."

As I reached to remove my shoes, Uncle Larry began to lay it down—explaining a worldview I hadn't known existed. In a quiet tone, he spoke of self-respect and how it meant nothing if you disrespected others—respect wasn't just saying "yes, ma'am" and "no, sir" to your elders. No, that's window dressing for people to hide behind. Even a hardened criminal guilty of heinous acts can have manners. Respect is honor and love. And love, Uncle Larry told me, is the lifeblood of this world, without which we are truly lost.

"We are all one family," he explained. "You love your family, even on the bad days." The greatest love any of us have, Uncle Larry continued to explain, is the love of our Maker. We have a responsibility to share what's in our hearts with others … not only the people we like or know, but everyone we encounter, no matter what challenges unfold on life's path. "It's got to be God first, family second, and everything else will fall in place. You hear me on this, if you hear nuthin' else, hear me."

I bent over to set my shoes next to Uncle Larry's, smiling a little. His loafers had to be at least twice the size of my sneakers. I straightened just as Uncle Larry dropped beside the bed to kneel.

"Join me." He reached out to touch my shoulder. "It's time for you to learn how to honor our Maker."

We knelt side by side on the floor, our hands folded before us, elbows resting on the side of Uncle Larry's bed. I was growing at a pretty steady clip by then, but down on the floor like that I had to stretch my back as straight as I could to get my elbows up on the bed. "Repeat after me: Our Lord, who art in heaven …."

I carefully enunciated every word, every line of the prayers he taught me. I did it to please Larry. He never steered me wrong. Big Larry was my mother's brother—big, strong and knowledgeable. Grandpa Ray was officially the man of the house, but long hours of physical labor left him little time for us kids, so Larry stepped in. And if Uncle Larry said it was important, it was. More importantly I recognized this was the start of a conversation with someone who could help me understand my path in life. God had always been a part of the daily conversation in our home, but I had yet to develop a one-on-one relationship. I simply didn't know how. I knew there was more to the world than the daily grind of the 'hood. I loved my family, my home … but it was a struggle to make sense of my life. I was too young to articulate my struggle to those around me. I thought about my brother, Tracy, and wondered whether Uncle Larry had the same conversation with him. Did Momma Cat know the prayer too? Did she say it every night as her brother said we should? I hoped she did … for her sake.

Uncle Larry repeated the prayers until he was confident I'd remember, and taught me to end each prayer with an "Amen." He said the words were nothing if you didn't speak from within, and told me I should always sit on the bed after nightly prayers and rub my feet together to remove any dust or dirt before getting all the way under the covers. I watched and listened, and promised myself I'd remember. I was concentrating so hard on getting it all in my head, it was several seconds before I realized Larry was laying across the bed, his arms behind his head, just smiling at me. The lesson was over. I grabbed my shoes and crossed the small room.

"Remember what we jus' did," Uncle Larry said. "And mean it from your heart."

To this day, I speak every syllable of my prayers directly from my heart.

Chapter 2
Mirrors

Sirens rang out in the distance. The sound traveled easily through the apartment's windows. Another crime in progress … just another hour in the 'hood. I wondered what new tragedy was unfolding on the streets of Perry Homes tonight. *Murder? Drug deal gone bad? Home invasion? Could be any one, or all of them.*

I sighed, dropping the washcloth I was using to wipe sticky goop from my face, and stared into the mirror. The only portion of the visage staring back at me I recognized was the eyes. My eyebrows and eyelids drooped into a frown. I strove for focus, to find some balance. My hands wouldn't stop shaking. I looked like a "dandified coon" in reverse—a warped parody of a blackface performer dripping tiny drops of vanilla ice cream all over the sink.

I backed toward the toilet and bumped my knee on the bathtub. "Maybe if I just sit for a minute," I said, realizing I sounded half-mad talking to myself.

A laugh erupted from the pit of my stomach and bubbled up my throat like bile. I sprang up from the toilet seat and headed back to the sink. My fingers gripped the sides of the basin so hard, I was sure my hands—or the sink itself—would shatter. I looked up in the mirror and came face-to-face with a mad man. *A madman,* I corrected myself. *Naw, man … a maaaad man.* The thought made me laugh even harder. Before I knew it, I was screaming.

* * * * * * * * *

Cat was up in our room humming to herself when I asked whether I could have some of the cake and ice cream in the fridge for dessert. When she responded, "Naw child, not tonight," I knew she had a few drinks in her. She still had a smile that lit up a room, the one that made her cheeks scrunch up and her eyes crinkle at the sides. The smile that often meant I was about to fall victim to a tickle attack. But there was also an edge to her tone. Her gaze hardened the longer I stood there.

Not to be thwarted in my quest for sugary goodness, I did what any other red-blooded almost ten-year-old kid would do—I went to ask someone else. As I padded across the hallway to Momzie and Grandpa Ray's room, I could already taste the thick frosting on the chocolate cake. When they said yes, I wasted no time heading down to the kitchen to grab my hard-won dessert.

It took everything I had not to stand in the kitchen gobbling down the cake and ice cream right there next to the stove. I possessed a world-class sweet tooth. Every day I ate at least five dollars-worth of crap food—honey buns, chocolate, cookies— anything containing obscene amounts of sugar I could get my hands on. Eager as I was to enjoy my chocolate cake and vanilla ice cream, I wanted to savor it. I cradled the bowl in my arm and headed upstairs to our bedroom.

Cat's eyes opened wide. She practically catapulted out of the bed as soon as she caught sight of me.

"You dumb red sum-a-bitch! Didn't I tell you, you couldn't have no damned cake and ice cream?" she screamed. Her cheeks flushed with anger. "How you gonna disrespect me like that? You didn't hear me when I told ya or what?!"

"Bu—bu—but, I, uh, I … ax. I did. Momma Rine said it was …." My voice failed me. She took a step closer, her hands raised.

My eyes clearly saw what was happening, but my brain refused to process it quickly enough to mount an effective defense. Violence in Perry Homes was nothing new—not even to a boy yet to enter high school. Our neighborhood didn't have the roughest reputation in Atlanta for nothing. All one had to do was step outside and wait a minute for someone to start a fight. My brother Tracy had come home bloody a few times. Heck, I'd even thrown some punches by his side. People fought over drugs, cars, girls, street cred, brand-name goods, you name it. Sometimes it seemed they fought just for something to do to take their minds off the grinding poverty and desperation plaguing them day after day after day. It was brutal—and it was normal. That was the harsh reality of the streets. That was life in Perry Homes.

But the life we lived outside wasn't the life we lived inside 579 Clarissa Drive. Tracy and I landed there off and on because Cat couldn't seem to raise us anywhere else. By the time I was seven my mother couldn't keep us anywhere at all, really. We moved around from place to place, with Cat uninterested, or unable to pay the bills, depending on her mood. Momzie and Grandpa Ray took us in permanently.

My grandparents' apartment was a place of hardship, hand-me-down clothes, and holes in the ceilings. Most of the clothes in the closet were only there because Momzie's employers gave her first dibs on their children's old stuff before throwing it out or donating it. Every single shirt I "owned" had someone else's name stitched into the back of it. Most of the underwear got quickly spoiled with skid marks. It didn't really matter much, most times the clothing stank from a lack of washing and stains became a secondary concern. Cat just wasn't real big on household chores.

Despite everything, Momzie made sure her home was filled with food and love. She could cook up a storm. It seemed like every time we walked past the kitchen, she was surrounded by pots and pans—elbows deep in a bowl of one of her favored meat and vegetable concoctions, adding spices that sent enticing aromas wafting through the living room and up the stairs. It was soul food at its finest. Dishes evolved from the hand-me-down scraps of food given to slaves by European slave traders and American slave owners until the ingredients became the backbone of black American cooking traditions. Chitterlings, collard greens, turnips, hog jowls, black-eyed peas, and squash stew—most dishes prepared with heaping lumps of lard because it was cheap and filling.

She may have been an average sized woman—about five foot four with a slender build—but my child's eyes saw Momzie as a giant, larger than life itself. She carried the weight of multiple generations on her sturdy shoulders, giving love to her children and their children in equal measure without reservation. She was never too busy to know instinctively when you needed a hug, a shoulder to lean on or a hand to cling to.

Momzie spent her days working as a housekeeper and child care provider for wealthier white and Jewish folk. Grandpa Ray worked at the tech steel manufacturing plant. Occasionally Momzie found work for Cat, cooking or cleaning at other people's homes and things would be good for a spell. But Cat never stuck with it. After a while, she'd stop showing up for work without an explanation. Around the same time her temper would get short. She grabbed me and Tracy, called us hurtful names. Momzie and Big Larry referred to these as her "dark periods," but I didn't really understand what they meant. All I saw was Momma Cat having a hard time. Okay maybe she hit the bottle a bit on the weekends and acted a little crazy, but so did the other adults in the house. Anytime she did go too far, I would take care of her.

Even angels have moments of doubt. A little bit of love always made things better.

That's not to say it was always easy. One night when she woke me at three in the morning to keep her company, I sure wasn't thrilled about getting out of bed. It was a Sunday night and I had school the next day. But Momma Cat needed me. She was hungry. I half sleepwalked downstairs to get her something to eat.

I struggled to reach the pot of neck bones on the stove, and get a bowlful of them into the microwave without dumping everything on the floor. At eight-and-a-half I hadn't really hit a growth spurt significant enough to reach the microwave buttons without using a chair. And to be honest I may not have done my best in the kitchen that night. I knew the food wasn't properly heated even before the glass bowl sailed over my head a few minutes later and neck bones splattered the wall behind me. Tracy woke up at the sound of the crash just long enough to take a dazed look around before closing his eyes again.

"You 'spect me to eat that cold ass shit?" Cat howled. I cowered away and scrambled to retrieve the bowl. "You stupid red blockhead fucka, take yo' lil stankin' ass back down there and get me some mo' and you do it right! And brang me the hot sauce like I said."

I cried all the way down the stairs. Through my tears, I clambered onto the chair and got her another bowl of food, making sure it was steaming hot. My tears followed me all the way back up to the bedroom. Momma Cat was right. I needed to try harder, do better. To win respect, you gotta be respectful. A cold bowl of food for your momma doesn't exactly qualify even if it is the middle of the night. The next time Cat needed something, I promised myself, I'd be perfect.

And now there we were a little over a year later, standing across from each other in our small bedroom with another bowl full of offensive food between us. Cat glared, her chest heaving. I stared back at her, afraid to blink, terrified to make even the slightest move.

Yeah, life in Perry Homes was tough and so was life inside 579 Clarissa. *But we were family.* The incessant violence ruling the street outside our door had no place inside the walls of our apartment.

I held my breath in an attempt to stop the stinging pressure of tears building behind my eyes. For a few seconds I thought it might actually work, until the first tear squeezed out of the corner of my right eye and slid down my cheek. *This is it.* I braced myself for the verbal lashing I knew was coming.

A gruesome smirk spread slowly across Cat's face, hardening her features right up to her bloodshot eyes—more a sneer than the smile she used to light up a room. When she spoke, she spat the words at me like boiling water jumping out of a teakettle—sizzling away in a rush of steam as each drop hit the stove.

"You want that ice cream more than you want to listen to yo' momma ... you ... you ... red ... blockhead sum-a-bitch?" she demanded, each word like a hammer on my ears. "You keep on like that, you dumb muthafucka. You ain't shit and you never gonna be nothin' in this world. Go on then. Go ahead and eat yo' damned cake and ice cream."

"Naw, it's okay," I replied, blinking through tears fighting one another for space on my cheeks. "I—I don't want it now."

"Oh naw, you want it. Ya wanted it bad enough to sneak behind my back, you blockhead muthafucka, ya gonna eat it. You gonna eat every goddamned bit of it or I'm gonna shove it down your stankin' ass fucking throat."

Cat hit me hard in the chest, knocking me off balance, and snatched the bowl from my hands. Holding my dessert over her head out of my reach, she pulled me hard by the T-shirt. Her nails tore through the worn material and scraped my chest. My legs buckled, leaving me to scramble alongside her on my knees. She dragged me away from the door, away from any possible hope of escape. With a hard shove, I found myself lying flat on my back on the other side of our bedroom.

Cat knelt, wedging her knees against my shoulder joints, locking down my arms. "You gonna see now what happens when yo' disrespect your momma, you dumb sum-a-bitch you." She gripped the bowl overhead with both hands.

I tried to close my mouth before the bowl smashed into my face. As soon as the first crumbs of cake hit my nose, I couldn't breathe. Thick frosting caught in my throat. All I smelled was chocolate. Cat ground the bowl as far into my face as physics would allow, twisting it left and right over my nose and mouth. She thumped the bottom of the bowl to make sure no cake or ice cream was left behind.

"How that taste, blockhead? You stupid muthafucka thought ya was gonna slide one past me. You keep on eating. There now, you eat it up," she said, leaning down and whispering in my ear.

I twisted my head away. The pressure on my chest was debilitating. I could barely breathe. Every time I managed to force globs of ice cream and cake out of my nostrils and mouth, they fell back in before I could get a full breath. I bucked my hips and kicked my legs, but couldn't get enough leverage to unseat her. After three unsuccessful attempts to free myself, I turned my attention back to breathing. A gooey clump of chocolate cake pieces mixed with a ball of ice cream slid toward the back of my throat. Cat's hand slipped and she lost her grip on the bowl long enough for me to cough the melting mess in my mouth back into the bowl and gulp in a quick breath. She grabbed the bowl again and forced the goop back between my lips.

I screamed so loud inside my head I thought my brain would explode. *Cat...please!* I prayed she would hear me and stop. Somewhere out there on the streets people were swaying to DeBarge's island rhythms or worrying their girl, like Eddie Murphy's, was only interested in partying all the time. In our apartment, I was dying. *Dying!* The taste of salt filled my mouth alongside the creamy vanilla of melting ice cream. *Tears*, I realized. I sobbed and choked again on a piece of cake.

Cat started giggling. She sat back, putting her full weight on my chest. "You eat it up now. You get every. Last. Bite," she told me and let go of the bowl.

The bowl slid off the right side of my face. I gasped for air. Melted ice cream was already beginning to dry on my skin, causing the bowl to catch and slide bit by bit toward the side of my neck. The bowl clattered to the floor.

Cat got to her feet. "Look at this mess you made. You gonna clean dis shit up, too. You red bastard."

I scrambled to my feet, blinking cake crumbs out of my eyes. Frosting and ice cream clung to my eyelashes, making them stick together. Cat stood, hands on hips, leering at me. I stood before her, my entire body shaking with the sobs I'd been unable to release with the bowl in my face, my fists balled up at my sides.

"Oh you a man now, aintcha? You gonna hit me, nigga?"

The desire to hit Cat consumed me. I shook with the desire to pay her back for the pain she'd put me through. *There*, I thought, eyeing the spot right next to her mouth on the left side where her skin puckered when she smiled. *Why shouldn't I?* I immediately regretted the thought.

Because she's your momma, and you have to respect your momma, an inner voice replied. It sounded a bit like Uncle Larry.

I paused, dimly aware of Cat clicking her tongue waiting for a response. I wanted to shout. *How could you do this, Cat?* Instead, I kept my silence. My shoulders slumped. I lowered my chin to my chest and closed my eyes.

"Naw. Uh-huh, I didn't think so," she said with a note of something like contempt in her voice. Cat turned her back on me, crawled into bed and went back to watching television like none of it ever happened.

* * * * * * * * *

I gulped in air and swallowed, wincing. My throat burned. I breathed through my mouth even though it felt like someone had rubbed sandpaper over the roof of my mouth and gums. Snot seeped out of my nose, spurred by my tears. It was hard to breathe and my screams were little more than whimpers, though they rang loud in my head. There wasn't anyone in the world fool enough to call someone a man when they were standing with ice cream and cake crumbs all over their face, tears welling in their eyes while they made sounds like a dog that's been kicked to the curb.

Ain't no place safe now. You better know it and abide. I released my death grip on the sink and grabbed the washcloth. As I worked to wipe the ice cream and cake goop off my face—pausing frequently to rinse out the sticky washcloth—I told myself how it was going to be now.

"Don't nobody luv me, but that's okay, 'cause I'm gonna be somebody," I assured the sad looking face in the mirror. With the right side of my face cleaned up, the left looked like it had a coating of partly dried wax on it. The strangeness of the image almost made me smile. "I ain't got nobody. I ain't got no daddy or nothin'. No need to worry now. They 'on't love me and that's okay, I 'on't need nobody to be somebody."

"I 'on't need nobody, cause I'm gonna be somebody." I repeated the phrase a few times to make sure my brain got the message. All around the neighborhood there were people who relied on no one but themselves to survive. Individuals who commanded respect, not on the basis of family relationships, but because of the power they held. *God helps those who help themselves.* Wasn't that what my elders said? Well then I was going to do just that.

* * * * * * * * *

To this day Big Larry jokes that when I was small I loved my momma so much, if she asked for a glass of water I'd fight anyone who tried to get it for her before I could. Most of the time the rest of the family would let me do it, rather than risk incurring the wrath of a precocious child.

Cat came and went whenever she pleased for as long back as I can remember. Sometimes we didn't see her for days—or even weeks—at a time. It hurt me when she'd leave. I was a quiet child to begin with, but when she was gone I'd get so quiet I was practically a mute until Cat returned. Everything changed after the ice cream incident.

After that night, I would learn what it meant to stand on my own, practice to attain the strength of independence. When I felt overwhelmed, I'd withdraw to the bathroom. Surround myself with cracked porcelain, rusty taps and a yellowed shower curtain that looked like someone had pulled it out of a thrift store one-cent bin, and stare into that mirror. It was my private time to express myself freely—my frustrations, anger, hopes and dreams. My chance to shed tears without family members asking, "Why you cryin', fool?" When I'd scream, Momzie, Grandpa Ray and Tracy wondered whether I'd lost my mind. And, sometimes, for just a few moments, I had.

The face in the mirror always brought me back. There had to be a purpose for my being here, something I was put on this Earth to do. I would take my moments, vent my rage and doubts, and live to fight another day. It didn't matter if nobody else saw the strength I saw in my face when I gazed into the looking glass. Someday they would know. And if they didn't? Well that was okay, because I didn't need anybody to be somebody. My independence was as clear to me as the gaze of the big brown eyes in the mirror.

Chapter 3
Mess o' Greens

I shut the apartment door behind me and waited for the inevitable request. There was always at least one member of our extended family at home during the afternoons. Tracy and I had school during the day, but once classes were finished, Tracy would plant himself in front of the television, or raid the refrigerator in preparation—if he wasn't at practice or out on the street messing around with his friends.

In between Grandpa Ray's shifts, I'd often come home to the soft thump, thump, thump of his plodding the short distance down the hall from his bedroom to the bathroom and back to lie down and rest. When I was greeted at the door by the smell of cologne—usually something woodsy or with hints of citrus—I knew Big Larry was around, but probably getting ready to go out.

I'd formed a habit of grabbing myself a sweet snack and some sort of drink—usually something just as sweet—to wash it down before settling in to do my homework. My routine was so well known within the family, many times the door had hardly clicked closed before someone would be yelling down the stairs for me to grab them something to drink, too. It always made me smile to be able to help.

With everyone coming and going with their own schedule it was rare to find all six of us home at the same time—except when Momzie was cooking a holiday meal. Momzie and Grandpa Ray worked during the weekdays; Cat, Big Larry, Tracy and I came and went pretty much as we pleased around our school schedule.

"Rob, that you?" Cat called.

"Yeah," I replied and waited to see what she wanted. Sweet tea was my first guess.

"Put your schoolbooks down and come right in here."

I took a few steps into the living room, and stopped. Momzie was sitting straight up in the recliner, her lips pursed, her hands folded neatly in her lap. She was dressed in her work clothes—a pair of black pants and a white blouse. Big Larry stood next to her, his elbow resting on the back of the chair. He met my eyes and nodded, but said nothing. Across from them two people sat on the couch with their backs to me.

As I rounded the side of the couch to get a better look, I found my brother sitting on the floor next to the glass coffee table. Tracy hugged his knees to his chest and stared down at the ground. He was pointing and flexing his feet, alternating left to right. Anyone who knew him well would immediately recognize it as a sign he was wound up or nervous about something.

A smile spread slowly across Cat's lips when she caught sight of me. Rays of sun coming through the window across from the couch where she sat played across her face, made her ebony skin glow. She'd applied a light touch of eye shadow that drew attention to her round brown eyes. The angles of her face stood out with her hair pulled back. She looked quite a bit like Momzie sitting across from her.

"Rob, yo' daddy is here to see you," Momma Rine said, breaking the silence.

I looked at the man next to Cat. He stood and held out his hand. He led me upstairs into the bathroom, leaving the quiet gathering behind us. I didn't want to be alone with a strange man. Who was he? Where did he come from? Was he really my father or pretending to be? He wasn't dressed fine enough to be from school or any sort of official agency. Neither Cat nor Momma Rine would send a representative of "the man" upstairs alone with me. That wasn't the kind of relationship any family in Perry Homes had with employees of government or agencies who worked with the poor.

"My name is James, and I'm yo' daddy," the man in the T-shirt and jeans told me. He walked into the bathroom and closed the toilet lid, indicating with a flip of his wrist for me to sit. As soon as he spoke, I was glad I was sitting. "I want you to repeat after me— James is my daddy."

I did what I was told.

* * * * * * * * *

I looked away from Cat to Momzie and Big Larry. Momzie's eyebrows were raised so high I thought they'd jump back behind her hairline. She studied her daughter's face, the force of the unasked question in her eyes rolling off her like heat off a furnace.

"Ya all set?" Cat asked softly, as James and I sat back down on the couch. "Now you know yo' daddy." There was no apology for the deceit or sudden appearance of my real father. No meaningful explanation, either.

In the silence that followed I tried to make sense of what had happened. The grownups in the room—which apparently included Tracy even though he was only a couple years my senior—were obviously privy to the revelation long before I was. I felt every eye on me, but said nothing. *How can this be my father?* I didn't understand. *Robert Jr. is my father.* Or so I thought. He was the man I was named after. Granted, Robert Jr. wasn't much of a father. I had only a few vague recollections of him; snapshot memories of singing songs and fights with Cat. But I knew my aunt, Robert's sister Diane, pretty well. I had been to Diane's house; she bought me sweaters on Christmas and a set of cars for my birthday a few years before.

James, I would later learn, had been heavily into drugs and drinking, spent some time in jail on drug charges—a man unfit to be a father in my mother's estimations. They dated for some time. Cat was already pregnant with me when they broke up and she started seeing Robert. Robert seemed like a better man, so she co-opted him for use as her baby-daddy. He'd never really wanted to be a family man. It was abundantly clear by his departure and general absence from most of our lives.

I figured it wasn't much of a loss. Plenty of the boys I knew in Perry Homes were growing up without fathers, or fathers who were in and out of the picture at irregular intervals. Maybe James was planning for this to be a new start; he would be a real father to me in ways Robert never wanted to be. I considered it briefly, until I looked around the room, from Cat, to Larry and finally Momzie. Every single one of them looked at me as if they were about to cry.

Only Tracy seemed unperturbed by the news that I had a new father. He had unwrapped his arms from around his knees and was playing with the shoelace on his left sneaker. Tracy's father wasn't around much either. Men come and go. That's how it was with Cat. Heck, that's the way it was with most folk we knew. I didn't understand what the big deal was. My dad, Robert or whoever, had never been a big part of my life. Uncle Larry was the closest I'd ever had to a father.

I could practically hear what Tracy was thinking, *Ain't nothin' gonna change.*

Momzie's children didn't have the same father either. Aunt Shirley and Aunt Pat had a different father than the remaining six children including Big Larry, Momma Cat, and my Aunt Brenda. Momzie worked two jobs for most of her life to take care of her brood. But they were still poor. Aunts Shirley and Pat's father made little effort to be a part of their lives. Grandpa Ray stuck around, but for a long time he wasn't the best help with the bills and child rearing. He would get paid on Thursdays and not come home until he was almost broke, usually on a Sunday. Momzie was forced to take shelter with her kin, living in the family's basement.

Eventually, around the time Momma Cat was nearing the end of her high school years, they got out of the basement and moved to Perry Homes. It wasn't much of a step up, for sure, but at least they had their own place. There were no picket fences, no station wagons. Heck, there wasn't even a yard or a driveway. But Momzie and her children stuck together, and did the best they could with what they had.

Would James break the absentee father pattern? Was I about to be blessed with something other than just a word—father—which meant little in the long run? *Daddy.* I tried it out in my head. It felt funny, but I figured it was okay, as it might not be something I ever called this man, James. I smiled a little and caught Momzie's eye. She tilted her head and smiled back, but her eyes were still watery.

James placed his hand on my arm. I turned and took my first good look at him. He had thick hair, cut short and neat. The round shape of James' face looked oddly familiar. He had a broad smile that took up much of what seemed like a welcoming face.

As I studied him, Momzie said, "Cat why don't you get som' to drank fo' everybody?"

James asked me about school and listened intently while I told him about spelling and math and history. I assured him I did my homework every night, and Tracy told him how good I was with arithmetic. We talked about Big Larry trying to teach us boys basketball, and hanging out at the Perry Homes recreation center. James told me a bit about his family—his momma and sister, his cousins, and the extended family in Texas.

"I'd like you to meet them all sometime," he said, and sipped the soda pop Cat brought out while we were talking.

He seemed easy enough to talk to, but how much was there to say to someone you don't know at all? I mean really. James was my father. Daddy. A stranger. I fell silent and thought about the family I knew—or thought I did—and the new one being thrust at me all the sudden. Around me, the grownups kept on talking—conversing about work, life, paying the bills and other adult topics holding no interest for a kid who just started the fifth grade.

I'd only ever called Cat "momma" one time in my life. It was at one of the many parties she went to with friends—soirees she would occasionally take me along to. She'd been leaning against a dishwasher talking with a small group of people when I made my approach. "You don' call me momma, ya call me Cat. Momma is what you call my mother," she'd instructed in a sharp tone.

Since then, anytime the word "momma" crossed my lips it was directed at Grandma Ethelrine—a term of affection which evolved into "Momzie" as I grew older. Not calling James "daddy" wouldn't amount to much of a change after living with Cat all my life.

I leaned around James and looked over at Tracy. My big brother gave me a wink. Besides Big Larry, Tracy was the only other male who truly took part in my life. He was outgoing and street smart in ways I would never be at age twelve. I was content to keep to myself most of the time, trying to figure out where I wanted to be and how to get there. Tracy was a creature who craved social interaction and wanted to thrive on the street. He had a thin build—not the most imposing figure for creating a reputation on the 'hood's rough streets. But he was intelligent, talked-fast, and used his God-given gifts to win people over with his quick wit and carefree smile. He was good at school. And whatever he said about my mathematical abilities, he could've just as easily said about himself. But whatever skill he displayed in his academic pursuits, they were secondary to Tracy's drive for prowess on the basketball court. Sports were his only real focus in terms of schooling—not books. They had tangible value for him. He took what he learned in the school PE classes and put it to use in street pickup games, using the knowledge and skill he possessed to gain position. I didn't need a report card to tell me my brother was smart.

* * * * * * * * *

"Knew you was gonna be here," Tracy said from the doorway to Momzie's bedroom. I looked up from my spot on the floor and found him gazing down at me, as if asking permission to come in.

I shrugged, figuring he'd come in whether I wanted him to or not. The muffled sounds of raised voices came from downstairs. They'd been at it for over an hour—ever since James left—and the grownups could talk to one another all night as far as I was concerned. I shifted lower to the ground, wedging myself securely between Momzie and Grandpa Ray's bed and the dresser where the television sat. Another half-hour or so and it would be time for *Knight Rider*.

Michael Knight was a "kool kat." And KITT was the baddest piece of machinery ever made. Tracy and I talked about KITT— who would be a better driver, and what special modifications we'd want if the vehicle were ours. Tracy was two years older and insisted—out of the two of us—if KITT came our way, he would be the main driver. He said he'd steer the sleek beast up and down the streets of Perry Homes, show everybody how it really was. Nobody in the neighborhood would mess with him ever again if he drove KITT. And if anyone got any funny ideas? He'd fire off the flamethrower every once in a while.

Tracy also had other things on his mind.

"So what ya think?"

I was surprised by the question. We were close, Tracy and me, we stuck together and looked out for each other on the street. We shared so many of the same experiences with the 'hood, with our mom—similar fears, anger and doubts. We had cried, sweat and raged together when Cat left us alone in a car for a couple hours with the windows rolled up one hot summer day. Cat brought us along when she and her male friend at the time headed to a run-down motel near old Fulton County Stadium to get high. She told us not to leave the car, and we didn't dare disobey no matter how scared we were. Tracy was about six years old; I was just four.

Heck, we even shared a bed—crammed on to a small contour sofa next to Momma Cat's bed in our crowded bedroom. Sometimes at night when I was having trouble falling asleep, I'd lie in the dark studying the hole in the ceiling above us. Visions of falling plaster or deformed creatures crawling out of the hole to scamper across the ceiling in search of victims would leave me shaky. But all I had to do was move a finger or a toe and I'd feel my brother lying next to me. In those moments having him close was a comfort.

Despite the physical proximity we had, and our automatic defense of each other against anyone looking to cause trouble, it was a rare occasion when we had any sort of deep, personal conversation. Sometimes when he would fall asleep before me, I'd risk a quick kiss on his cheek. I loved and admired my brother. Still, Tracy had his way to do things, and I had mine. There just wasn't a lot of tenderness in our lives. We were too poor to afford it.

For a moment I toyed with the idea of pretending not to know what he meant, but decided against it.

"He seemed a'right."

"Yeah?"

"Yeah," I said firmly.

"Yeah ... maybe he'll be good for some new clothes or somethin'."

Chapter 4
Personal Playbook

Samuel Culbreth was a giant. He was a big guy physically, even as a teenager, but what made him huge was his football prowess. In Perry Homes if one thought of football, a picture of Big Sam knocking people down like bowling pins was the mental image that popped up. When I heard he was going to be at the Perry Homes Recreation Center—the Rec Center—doing his thing on the field, I headed over for what would ultimately be the first of countless hours on the gridiron.

As soon as I got my hands on the pigskin, I knew football was meant for me. It was a regulation size football, deep brown leather with white laces. When I pressed my hands together around the ball it gave a little, but it was tough, built to take a hit and keep its form. This particular ball looked like it had seen quite a few rough games. There were scuff marks on the faux leather and somebody had scrawled black lines alongside the white laces. It was beautiful.

When the volunteer rec center coach, Coach Price, told me to take a handoff and run, I found a clear path to a defined goal—a way of thinking about progression and framing a strategy previously unknown to me. Right down the field, was the end zone. My goal? Take the ball, work with my teammates and get across the line. The idea was clear and concise. Of course, getting to the goal meant successfully passing a bunch of guys looking to pummel our side into the ground. It would be no easy feat to get through them. The rec center game was similar to pickup football and a lot of guys were only there to deliver as hard a hit as they could. But I could see the goal I needed to meet and the pathway laid out right in front of me. I knew exactly what I had to do.

Rec center games were usually divided into age groups, younger kids playing other younger kids, and the high school-aged guys playing other high schoolers. On this particular day, everybody was playing together in one game. It wasn't much of a surprise to see older kids putting some serious hurt on the younger ones. I'd like to say I was the exception, but I wasn't. I got knocked down so hard, so many times in the first few minutes of play there was a part of me thinking it would be better to lie on the field for a while and let them carry on without me. The larger, more determined part of me knew I had to carry on. I couldn't lay down and let the goal slip away after hitting a few snags in the process. I was going to help my team play the best game it could and drive the football toward the end zone.

I grabbed the ball again and looked downfield for a clear path. After nearly an hour of playing, I felt muscles aching I didn't know I had. Yet even though I knew there would be some soreness to deal with later, I was exhilarated. *I was in control.* I could, by my own actions, be in charge of my own success. There was a slight hole to the left side of the quarterback and if I was quick enough, I could sprint through to open ground. I made my move … and ran smack dab into Culbreth. I found myself kissing the grass. He didn't get a reputation for success on the field for nothing.

The hit was so hard it felt like every organ in my body jumped three inches to the right. They only began to shift back to their proper locations when I rolled over and slowly rose to my feet. Once up, I realized the tackle hadn't really moved any organs around, but it had moved my bowels.

I hated to leave. Football was fun and felt more natural to me than basketball or any other extracurricular activity I'd tried. The patterns and forms for success—simultaneously depending on the law of probability and unknown actions of others on the field— were fascinating. The goal was always there. The players had to find a way to achieve it. And I knew I could. But after facing walls covered in graffiti and dried feces during a quick visit to the rec center's bathroom—the kind of place even cockroaches couldn't use without feeling dirty—I asked Coach Price if I could go home instead to take care of my business.

I looked around the neighborhood and walked quickly as I could with my cheeks clenched and jaw locked. It helped keep my mind off the bubbling, percolating sensation running across my stomach toward the small of my back.

Perry Homes had been built in 1959 as one of several public housing projects constructed by the city of Atlanta in the second half of the twentieth century. It was built for the poor, and the poor inhabited it. Located on the city's northwest side, Perry Homes quickly gained notoriety for loud music, street thugs and fast cars. By the time I became a full-time resident in the early 1980s, Perry Homes was well on its way to having enough criminal stats to fill the record rooms of numerous police departments in the city. Crime was the 'hood's main form of commerce, and business was good.

Every building in Perry Homes looked almost identical—two stories tall with red or brown brick facades. Apartments there were ground floor units with two-floor interiors. There weren't any porches to speak of, only small slabs of concrete outside the front doors. It was industrial, sterile. Anyone driving by Perry Homes might think it was made up of barrack structures from a decommissioned army base.

Folks took to putting chairs outside their front doors—not anything fancy, just the white plastic kind from a discount store. There wasn't any point in putting something nicer than that out, somebody would just steal it. Residents sat outside their front doors day after day, watching the comings and goings of fancy cars few could afford, but an awful lot of people seemed to have. The roads crisscrossed the front and rear of the buildings, much like the telephone wires running overhead. Small children played in groups on the sidewalks and in the grassy areas behind buildings, running in between the lines of laundry strung between the trees to dry.

The thousand or so families living in the barrack-style buildings of Perry Homes did so with little distraction. There were no movie theaters in Perry Homes. No record stores, no Sears & Roebuck's, or restaurants. We had the rec center, a public library, a small arcade, a welfare office, and a couple mom-and-pop shops. There were a few churches nearby on the streets outside the neighborhood.

In the 1990s, as Atlanta was preparing to host the Olympics, the city began moving residents out of Perry Homes. They started demolishing it in 1999, and replaced Perry Homes with nearby West Highlands, which opened in the summer of 2004. City officials praised community and business leaders for coming together to replace a "blighted community" with smart-looking single-family homes, rental apartments and a senior community. Shirley Franklin—Atlanta's Mayor when West Highlands opened—touted it as a great example of a model development that would change people's lives.

Momzie and Grandpa Ray ended up in the West Highlands area. Each visit to see them over the years after Perry Homes was destroyed, I saw less and less evidence our old neighborhood even existed. When I go back now, the area is full of trees and grass. No buildings, no streets, only memories. The hills that ran through Perry Homes are the only remaining landmarks from one of the more ferocious areas Atlanta has known in the last century.

The day of the rec center game, I took a shortcut home, cutting across the parking lot and picking my way through our favorite hilly path instead of walking down Drew Drive and Kerry Drive to get to Clarissa. It wasn't an official hiking path. The only marker was the worn trail made by kids wading through the grass and rocks. If you walked through at night and didn't know the way, you'd probably break an ankle, but we kids new every low hanging branch and each dip along the way. Most of us could close our eyes and traverse the path without missing a step if we really needed to.

When we were little and visited Momzie and Grandpa Ray, sometimes Tracy and I would join the neighborhood kids, like my buddy Teo, in games of tag or hide-n-seek. Teo—a quick-witted boy, good with jokes—was my sidekick and I was his. He was the only guy I ever invited over for a sleepover after he begged me to do it. Sleepovers in our crowded, roach-infested apartment weren't top on my list of things to do. It was too embarrassing, but Teo was my boy. From the first day of kindergarten on, we were close—battling each other in video game competitions, exploring the rolling hills and concrete patchworks of Perry Homes, planning our future. For many of the kids we played with, the future was short.

Teo died a few years later in 1994 on Bankhead Highway. He lost control of his vehicle and collided with another car during an apparent street race. He killed himself and the woman driving the other vehicle. The same year I watched in horror as the life slipped out of my football teammate, Marcus—shot in the head over drugs or a girl. We never did know for sure. Only thing we did know, we were absolutely powerless to do anything but watch a gloppy mess of his blood and brains spread across the pavement. My buddy Dexter—who we called Deck—was abducted along with two others, tied up, tortured, and killed execution style a couple years after Marcus died. Big Dave was killed alongside his uncle in a botched drug deal.

Even though a lot of children used the path, it was usually quiet. I would occasionally step off the path to sit beneath a tree and eat the plums I picked from it. From there, I'd look up at the rays of sun cutting through the leaves, think about a day's adventures, or talk to my Maker and ask for His guidance.

About halfway through the path, just as the buildings of Clarissa Drive came into view, my stomach gave a massive jolt. I hurried through the tall grass, practically speed-walking toward the street and the realization hit: *I'm not going to make it.* No sooner had the thought crossed my mind, my bowels released a warm cascade into the back of my jeans. It made its way down the back of my legs with frightening speed.

I continued forward, clenching as best I could to keep matters from getting any worse. I stepped out on to Kerry Drive, fighting to keep a scream of frustration from exploding out of my mouth. Up ahead and off to the right, groups of people were on the street. I almost bolted when I realized one of the groups was made up of Chiquita, Charles and other classmates from school.

I scoured my panicked brain for a way to get home without actually having to interact with them.

A small child called out, "Look! Chocolate!"

I knew the horrible truth before I turned to see the young kid pointing at me. My secret shame was about to become public.

I don't want to be known as the "doo-doo" boy. There has to be a way out of this. My heart beat-boxed in my chest. *Stop and think, Rob.* I knew what the goal was—home. I needed to develop a strategy to get there.

I trolled through my memories of lessons learned, hoping for something to help me out of this mess. Big Larry never gave me any schooling on what to do when you're standing in the middle of the street with feces dripping into your shoes. Once I found a way out of this, I promised myself I wasn't ever going to tell Big Larry about this particular adventure.

And Daddy? Well, as far as I could remember the only wisdom he ever shared was … a toothbrush.

Earlier in the year, we'd traveled cross-country to the great state of Texas for one of his family member's wedding. It was the only time after learning he was my father we spent any time together. We stopped at a gas station in Alabama and he said, "I'll buy you whatever you want." I grabbed a lollipop and an oatmeal pie.

"I want you to take this, too." James leaned down to hand me a toothbrush. "No matter what you do in life, son, you brush your teeth."

Yeah, I don't think that toothbrush is big enough to deal with this, Daddy. I started to giggle, but stopped when I slapped my thigh and heard a squelching sound.

Bolting for the apartment wasn't going to work. People would think I was either running away from or to something, and with my luck I'd end up with a bunch of people following me home asking questions. Staying put in the middle of the pavement wouldn't work, either. Talking was a great pastime when you've got nothing else for entertainment. There was a lot of talk in Perry Homes. If I stayed in one spot, it wouldn't be long before some well-meaning passerby would start a conversation.

There was only one thing to do. I rearranged my features into the toughest look an eleven-year old could manage, dropped my head to my chest, and marched across the street. I kept my lips pursed, my eyebrows furrowed, and stared straight ahead to let anyone I passed know I didn't have time for idle chat. I felt like every eye in Perry Homes was on me. But truth be told, I don't think anyone—besides the young boy who thought I'd smeared my afternoon candy snack across the seat of my pants—had a chance to notice my predicament on my purposeful march home.

To say there were no tears as I cleaned myself off in the bathroom would be a lie. I finished cleaning up with a thorough hand and face washing, and examined myself in the mirror. I added some valuable lessons to my mental playbook that day.

Brush your teeth. It was good advice. It was also the only real advice I'd get from James. I would not see or hear from him again until well into my adult years, except for a single phone call when I was a teenager so he could request my social security number for tax purposes.

What I learned on the football field could be applied in life. *Define the goal, craft a strategy, and execute.* Sure, there was always going to be someone or something out there looking to knock you down. Not every drive would result in a touchdown. And yeah, sometimes you might encounter unpredictable situations.

It's all a part of the game, remember that. I was still learning. And I couldn't wait to get my hands back on a football.

Chapter 5
The Fish Plate Hustle

Momzie's reputation extended well beyond the borders of Perry Homes. On the weekends, there was a parade of folks pulling up in front of 579 Clarissa looking to fill their bellies. "I want the works, Miss Rine," they'd say, practically shoving money in to Momzie's prematurely aged hands. Years of housework left the skin on her hands papery and wrinkled, her joints swollen from heavy use. But boy could she cook up dishes that left you salivating for more.

For four dollars and twenty-five cents, folks got two pieces of whiting fillet with French fries and a salad. And for just a dollar more, customers could buy themselves a plate with fried chicken instead of fish.

Man, she was rolling in cash by the end of the weekend. But it went nearly as fast as it came thanks to Momzie's fondness for playing the numbers—Cash 3, lotto. You name it, she was playing. As far back as I can remember, she'd drop forty dollars a day trying her luck. She never won big. And so she hustled—out the door every weekday morning to care for other people's children and nicer homes, and in the kitchen all weekend long, face wet with perspiration, moving from dropping fresh batches into the fryer to setting up plates with the food ready for people to buy. As the rest of the family came and went throughout the weekend, Momzie conscripted us into helping her serve. If we did a good job, we might pick up a couple of bucks at the end of the day.

Movers and shakers, that's what we were. Plenty of breadwinners in Perry Homes worked a nine-to-five, dealt drugs, or waited for the monthly government checks and were content. But that wasn't the way it worked at 579 Clarissa. We may not have had much, but we earned every bit of it. There wasn't a member of the Singleton household not looking to get theirs every single day.

For the most part our home businesses were legal-ish activities, like Momzie's plates. I would take chips and candy Momzie provided—thanks to her early morning trips to warehouses—with me to sell at school. I made between thirty and forty dollars a day cashing in on the snack desires of my fellow students. At the end of the week, Momzie gave me a cut of the earnings—usually about twenty-five dollars.

I also got a cut of the monthly welfare check—fifty bucks. Momma Cat received over two hundred dollars, plus about the same amount in food stamps. She kept most of it to support her habits, selling the food stamps for cash. The income enabled her to avoid seeking proper employment. Later, after Tracy turned eighteen, Momzie convinced Cat to give me the entire check—which was reduced to around one hundred dollars because Tracy was no longer a minor.

Cash in my pockets was great, but it wasn't nearly enough for a twelve-year-old with dreams of designer jeans, a Starter jacket, and the best football equipment money could buy.

Problem was, there weren't a lot of options for earning more.

Tracy went to a high school outside Perry Homes, a change expanding his sales possibilities by a huge margin. In the 'hood the bulk of business involved selling drugs. There was plenty to go around. There was also plenty of competition. High school kids, Tracy learned quickly, weren't interested in the kind of candy manufactured by Hershey's or Mars. It was only a couple of weeks into the school year before he embraced a new kind of business opportunity and branched out from selling edible snacks to the kind you could smoke.

Most of the time Tracy and Big Larry got their smack from Shorty—or 'Shawty' as we called him—a neighborhood kingpin with enough business savvy to offer his client dealers options. Shawty sold his rocks as eight balls for one hundred and twenty five dollars or as two-for-one dime bags for those looking to turn quick sales. Tracy and Larry preferred the former. They huddled together in Big Larry's bedroom to divvy up the product and keep Momzie and Grandpa Ray from knowing about their activities. I didn't think they had much to fear from the family. Momzie and Grandpa Ray kept busy with work, to the point of collapse most days. Momma Cat was MIA whenever she found a new man to call her boyfriend. Even when she was around, Cat didn't seem to care much about what we might be doing. Whenever Cat appeared interested in their activities, Tracy and Big Larry would give her a few rocks to keep her busy. Ever since we moved in with Momzie and Grandpa Ray—and even before then—Cat left our parenting to other members of her family.

It had been almost five years since Momzie received a call from our old neighbors. Back when Tracy, Cat and I were living on our own. "You better go check on those boys," the woman told Momzie. When she arrived, the door was closed to her. Momma Cat put the fear of God into us about opening the door when she was gone. After several minutes—during which Momzie pleaded, cajoled, and unleashed a couple threats of her own—Tracy risked Cat's wrath and opened the door. Momzie took us home and fed us. We ate. And we ate. And we didn't go back. A short while later our mother came to join us at Momzie's—and there we stayed. Momma Cat hadn't paid much attention to what we did when we lived under a roof she commanded. I didn't think Tracy and Big Larry had much to worry about from her now.

With the precision of mechanical engineers, Tracy and Big Larry placed rocks on a record album cover and carefully made cuts using a razor blade. They could get as many as thirty dime-bags from an eight ball—which seemed like a hella good return on investment if you asked me. Occasionally they'd let me and my cousin Lil' Larry sit on the edge of the bed and bag up rocks for sale.

But Big Larry didn't like it. "You be better off concentratin' on those schoolbooks, boy. This ain't for you," he'd tell me. It was practically a mantra for him. "This ain't for you." I took him at his word.

Big Larry was, and remains, a dapper don. When he stepped out he looked and smelled fine—like a new car pulling off the sales lot for the first time. His closet was full of colorful silk suits, polo shirts, and button downs. His dresser top was crowded with cologne, jewelry, and hats. Throughout the long hot summer months, Larry had a stable of cargo shorts in khaki, gray, and tan to choose from. They showed a good portion of his long lean legs. He'd pair the shorts with T-shirts or polos, leaving just enough of his impressive guns visible. Many times I'd sit on the edge of his bed and watch in awe as he got ready to go out with one of the many women who always seemed to be circling 'round.

"What you lookin' at, sonny boy?" he'd ask with a smile whenever he caught sight of me in the mirror.

He thought out loud a lot while he was getting ready, talking about hard work, honesty, family, and the dangerous lure of the streets. I listened intently. I knew his ruminations were meant for my benefit; but on more than one occasion my mind wandered in a different direction. I wanted to be Big Larry—tall, strong, capable, respected ... desired. I prayed to our Maker for guidance, weighed Big Larry's words, and hoped I'd find a way.

I was pretty proud when I landed my first "real" job. I wasn't going to make the kind of money Tracy, Big Larry, or Momzie were pulling in with their ventures, but I was a bona fide earning man at age twelve. That was the way it should be. A man's got to earn his keep, no matter how old he is.

Kurt, the Youth Opportunity Unlimited of Georgia program driver, never said much while us kids scrambled into the back of his raggedy brown van. He would drive around the city of Atlanta, dropping us off one by one at various locations boasting steady retail foot traffic. He'd give a nod and a quickly spoken promise to come back for us in a few hours. Many times, I ended up in a northern Atlanta plaza with a Kroger grocery store, a couple of restaurants, and an Athlete's Foot among the half-dozen or so retailers. Some of them didn't seem to stick around for very long.

"I'm with the Y.O.U. of Georgia program. The Y.O.U. of Georgia program is a special work and activity program that helps keep young people like me off the streets and out of trouble," I'd tell the folks I managed to stop before entering or exiting a store, or their vehicle. "We have a special event for this year and with your purchase of any one of my items, it can help me to win a trip to Washington, D.C."

Between customer interactions I'd rehearse my script, testing out different tones and intonations best suited to reflect my earnest desire to make a sale. Talking to people was second nature after honing my retail skills at home and school. There wasn't anyone on the street peddling those boxes of chocolate mint patties, peanut brittle, and chocolate nut clusters like I could. By altering the pitch of my voice and my speech, depending on the individual I was interacting with, I could study people's responses—and make the tough sales. When I hit it just right, sometimes I'd come away with a nice tip, too.

I rushed upstairs to our room after every shift to count my take. Candy cost three dollars and fifty-five cents a box and we received a fifty-cent cut. On a good weekday I'd come home with about ten dollars. On the weekends I was earning twenty big ones. It was hard work, but I was earning by my own accord. Didn't have to wait on anybody to buy me a pair of jeans or some new shoes. Every few months I'd head downtown to Kessler's—a small family-owned chain of department stores—and pick up something special for myself. It was brand-name stuff at bargain basement prices, perfect for a man on his way up. Levi's jeans were my favorite purchase. They were paper Levi's, not the best quality, so I'd spend extra time with the iron, putting a real sharp crease on the legs of every pair I owned.

It didn't take long for me to realize, while I was earning money all on my own, it wasn't enough for me to earn the respect I needed to take my place in the hierarchy of the 'hood. I was beginning to get bigger than most the kids my age, with broad shoulders and muscular thighs. It was my size—maybe a few words from Tracy or Big Larry, or my family members' reputations—keeping me from getting regularly challenged to fights. I was still a little kid needing protection in the eyes of the streets, and I knew I could do better. Still, I stuck with the candy selling. I suffered sore feet and sporadic shifts for about a year and half before moving on to bigger and better things. As fate would have it, that was around the time Kurt from Y.O.U. stopped coming around Perry Homes. Word in the 'hood was he ran into some trouble with the police and the kids weren't working for him anymore.

Chapter 6
Blacky Moves In

Momma Cat was at it again. Lying in the dark next to Tracy, I could make out the dimmest of outlines in the bed next to ours. They had the blankets pulled almost all the way up to their shoulders, but I could see his head and her arms around his neck. Cat and her boyfriends were usually pretty good about being quiet during their nocturnal activities. Another giggle escaped her lips and I winced. It wasn't loud, but it had a shrill, high-pitched tone—the kind she got when she'd been hitting the junk. I didn't need the noise to tell me, though. The rank odor of alcohol wafted over from her bed to ours. I guessed it was beer—a smell I knew all too well.

I pinched my nose shut and yanked on the blanket Tracy hogged, pulling it up to my eyeballs. I wondered what Cat had been ingesting in the two days before she returned an hour or so ago, and guessed from her behavior it was a combination of crack and various kinds of alcohol.

She used to take me with her to parties. We spent our weekends hanging out together. I helped get people drinks when they needed them, and averted my eyes when they got to cursing and other lewd behavior. The grown-ups always said I was a good boy. Cat was proud of me. She'd unleash a tickle attack on my arms and belly, or reach over to ruffle my hair during the parties—letting me know she was glad I was there. Sometimes Momma Cat would need a little help putting the key in the lock when we got home or getting up to the bedroom to sleep it off. It was our time together, just me and her.

About two years before, she stopped taking me to parties. I still wasn't sure why. The question nibbled at me every time she went away. And she went away a lot nowadays. Not just on the weekends, either. If she had a steady man at the time, we'd hear about her staying at their place. For the most part, we didn't know where she was or what kind of drugs and drinking she was doing. Every now and then, she was so out of her senses when she came back, Momzie and Big Larry were likely to find themselves ducking a wild swing instead of getting a straight answer out of her. Cat didn't start swinging because they asked her what she'd been doing. Oh no. She'd come home reeling after days of partying, asking for money. When she got a no or the suggestion perhaps she might want to sleep instead of going back out, sometimes it went bad. A few months earlier, Momzie refused Momma Cat's request for money and turned from the sink-full of dishes she was washing to find Cat coming at her with a baseball bat. Afterward Momzie couldn't remember exactly how she got the bat away from Cat, or how she ended up with her hands around her daughter's neck, ready to wring it good. The next morning Momzie was devastated when it became apparent Cat only vaguely remembered the encounter. She embraced her daughter with a broken heart.

Cat proclaimed, "It wasn't me momma. It was Blacky. Blacky be on my chest, doin' these things."

My relationship with Cat changed after the ice cream encounter, but I missed our time together. I even missed the silly tickle attacks; they annoyed me as much as they made me laugh. I hated to admit the Momma Cat I saw sporadically now was someone I really didn't want to spend time with. But I'd rather have her home fussing and giving us all headaches, than turning on the news to hear her body had been pulled out of a garbage dumpster.

A particularly loud grunt jolted me from my thoughts. The man with Cat groaned, "Oh yeah." They seemed like they were having fun.

I sighed, recalling my first encounter with a girl and shuddered at the memory playing out in excruciating detail in my head like a film.

* * * * * * * * *

Shondra was a good-looking girl. I lay spread across the couch, waiting for whatever pleasure we were about to engage in. She'd transferred to our school a couple of years before and had her eye on me for a while. "Come on, let's do it," or sometimes, "Take me into the woods," she'd say. But it wasn't until well into seventh grade when I found the guts to take her up on the offer and brought her home one day after school. Shondra had experience. She was my age, but dating an eighteen-year old. I couldn't fathom the things she'd already learned.

I glanced up and found her looking down at me with a hungry look in her eyes. She had dimples and piercing brown eyes. She looked at me like a street cat that'd spotted dinner. My body responded to her hunger as my gaze traveled down to her chest. She had the biggest tits I'd ever seen.

Cat had noticed and taunted me whenever she caught sight of Shondra. "That girl got some big ol' tiddies."

"A'right now, whatcha gonna do?" Shondra quipped, tossing out her left hip and putting her hands on her waist.

"Yeah, let her know what time it is, man." Tracy chimed in.

For a moment I had forgotten Tracy was keeping a lookout at the bottom of the stairs in case Momzie, Grandpa Ray, or Big Larry decided to come down for anything. Grandpa Ray rarely came out of his room once he'd retired for the evening. However, the sexual escapades of my cousin Lil' Larry a couple months earlier had caused a pretty major blowout. Ray, the family tattletale, walked into the living room and turned on the light to find Lil' Larry and a girl doing it on the couch. Without a word, he turned the light off and went back upstairs. Less than a minute later, Momzie came flying downstairs in a rage, unleashing a tongue-lashing on the youngsters with the force of a category-three hurricane. There wasn't a single member of the family who wanted to be in the path of her storm again.

Tracy was practically dancing in and out of the hallway—popping around the corner and clucking his tongue. I struggled to come up with a response. I knew he was trying to think of something, too.

"You need some help, little bro? She fine and I'm ready if you ain't," he taunted.

I glowered at him. Slight movements out of the corner of my eye made me turn my attention back to Shondra. She was unbuttoning her pants. Blood coursed through my body, and my groin began to twitch when her pants hit the floor.

Her underwear followed. I gasped. *She has pubes!* My cheeks flushed and my member returned to a resting state. I was painfully aware of the fact that I didn't have any fur down there to impress her with. It was a big deal for us seventh and eighth graders. Many of the boys were already developing into men. Those of us who hadn't yet pulled hairs from our heads, cupped them in our fists, stuck our hands in our pants, and pulled them out to prove we weren't falling behind. *She's going to laugh at me, tell everyone at school, Rob ain't got nothin'.* I fought to stay in the moment, to do what was expected of a man in this kind of situation.

She told the girls she was coming to my house when we headed out after football practice. "A'right, a'ight, I'm goin' over to Robert's house and we gonna do it." I was scared. Shondra came closer, putting her hands and lips on me.

In a panic, I babbled about my grandmother being home and needing to make sure she didn't hear or see anything. Shondra reminded me Tracy was standing guard. I said I might need a glass of water before we got started. Shondra dug her fingers into my shoulders and shook her head no.

"I—I—hold up. I ain't ready yet," I squeaked. "I need to use the bathroom real quick."

I practically shoved her off me and jumped up to beat a hasty retreat toward the upstairs bathroom. I felt their eyes on my back the entire way. As I shut the door, I heard Shondra and Tracy giggling.

I knew I had to find a way to deliver on the promise that brought Shondra to our home or Tracy would do it in my place. He already had a couple girls he was talking to and he was only two years older. In Perry Homes "real" men had multiple girls on call. Some girls, the slutty ones, might be going with a couple guys or be available for anyone's use. But men, "real" men, had a stable of their own—girls who picked up the phone only for them and offered them some sugar.

I worked my thing like a sailor stuck at sea without a woman within a thousand miles. I may not have fully developed yet, but I wasn't going to have Shondra spreading it around the neighborhood that I couldn't even do the deed. I would never live it down. After several minutes, I was ready to go and I bolted back downstairs to the living room where Shondra was lying on the couch, one leg dangling off the side.

She smiled and opened her arms. I strode over to mount her. I laid there on top of her, my equipment next to hers, still uncertain how this worked. I started grinding on her like the other boys at school and I did when we walked up behind girls.

"Ya gotta put it in. It's gotta go in," Shondra said and grabbed ahold of me and showed me where to go.

Tracy popped around the corner again. "Whatcha doin'? Whatch'all doin'?"

Shondra replied for both of us.

"I think it's gonna take two of y'all to handle this stuff. Should we let him?" She laughed.

I cringed and pumped even harder.

"What you need me to do? You need some help over there, little brother?" Tracy crept farther into the room.

"Shondra, you want me to come over there?" he added and burst out giggling.

"Yeah, I'm gonna need both o' y'all cause this, ri'here, real good," she called back to him. "That's all ri' with me."

As good as it felt to be taking care of my business the way a man's supposed to, I found it hard to look at Shondra's face. Each time I caught her eye, she was sucking her thumb and turning her head back and forth. She kept looking at Tracy and winking, silently asking, "You next?" I stopped looking and relied on her occasional moans and grunts to let me know whether I was doing it right. After a couple minutes, Shondra told me to stop. She was done. I did so gladly, celebrating inwardly. *I did it!*

The relief was somewhat short-lived. Word spread around school, I had no fur. "Rob, you bald-headed," the kids teased. It hurt pretty bad, but I played it off. After all, Shondra had done me the favor of letting people know my "thang" was ample and in fine working order. It wasn't ideal, but it was a lot better than I had feared.

The next time I wouldn't be the student, I would be the teacher. And girls would learn to respect me properly.

* * * * * * * * *

The lips of an angel, I remembered wistfully.

I listened to the sounds coming from the other bed. They were breathing in tandem—his throaty snores coming opposite Cat's deep breaths. I strained to focus on Momma Cat and tune out the noises of the man I'd met a couple hours ago, but whose name was already as foreign to me as a plate of escargot. *That used to be me.* I remembered the nights when Tracy, Cat, and I would share a bed together—me cuddling up close to Cat to put my head on her shoulder and find comfort in the rhythmic rise and fall of her chest. I felt the prickly sting of tears building behind my closed eyes and swallowed hard, forcing them down.

Cat was giving her love, or at least her version of it, to others now. It never stuck. There was a series of men, loud arguments, beatings, and more scars than I could begin to count, or comprehend. What I did know, I never wanted to see Cat curled up in her bed clutching a towel filled with ice and soaked in Witch Hazel against her face, as I had a few months prior.

Her hyper-dramatic on-again, off-again relations with one of Big Larry's bag boys—Doo Dirty—had erupted into violence. The result was a head so swollen it looked like a melon. If I had seen the beaten woman walking down the street, I wouldn't have recognized her as my mother. Bruises and cuts were not unusual for Cat. Generally, she'd patch herself up or slap on some makeup and get on with her life. She couldn't do that this time. A rage I could barely control consumed me when I beheld her battered face. If I were able to get my hands on Doo Dirty, I would kill him. Whatever had happened between me and Cat, however damaged our relationship might be with the presence of Blacky, she was *my* mother and I loved her. Even if I had little desire to spend much time with the woman she had become.

Blacky was living with us full-time now. Maybe not that night, though. No, Cat had been happy, smiling, giggling. Despite her euphoria, there was a steely glint in her eyes when she told me and Tracy to lie quietly in our bed and go to sleep. Neither of us thought to question the strict order. Many nights now, too many, the charming woman who sang in ethereal tones capable of rocking your very being, was replaced by a wild-eyed and violent lost soul. A vicious beast bent on the destruction of those around it—parent and child alike. I didn't know why her drinking and drug use had gotten so out of control, or where this other personality came from. She was losing control of herself over to a being called Blacky.

I love you, Cat, I told her silently, and wished I could climb into her bed and give her a hug. Those days were gone. She may never have said it, but she didn't have to. I was old enough to see the differences in our lives.

Chapter 7
Middle Class Living

Misty Waters. The name conjured images of a clean clear lake surrounded by towering trees and a rainbow of wildflowers as far as the eyes could see. Of water so still it looked like glass in the early morning when the sun rose above the treetops, sending warm rays of light on the landscape below. It was a place where nothing bad could happen as long as you were careful not to startle or disturb any wildlife calling the heavenly place home.

I loved it there.

Misty Waters didn't actually have a lake. It did have basketball and tennis courts, a swimming pool, and lots of green grass. The housing development was a few miles outside downtown Decatur, an in-town Atlanta suburb known for its historic sites and trendy festivals. It had none of the antiseptic feel of Perry Homes' barracks and poorly paved streets. Misty Waters was full of the sounds of laughing children, the cheers and boos accompanying neighborhood pickup games, and the chatter of hardworking Southern women taking breaks from cooking and cleaning to enjoy a bit of sun.

It was middle class living to my child's eyes. I stayed there every weekend I could and most of the summers from the time I was eight until I started high school. On the one occasion I returned as an adult, I found chipped sidewalks, overflowing dumpsters, and loose railings in the stairwells of Misty Waters—now known as Spring Valley. The laughter of children had been replaced by taunting and shouting from teenagers and older men chilling out in their wife beaters, baggy jeans hanging precariously halfway down their backsides. Womenfolk gently pulled visitors away from the groups, tossing snide remarks about the beverages the men held concealed in brown paper bags. They told harrowing tales of a growing gang presence and deadly violence.

But that's not the Misty Waters I loved.

Grandma Bea—Beatrice—had a nice apartment there she shared with her daughter, my paternal aunt Mary, and her grandson John. There wasn't a lot of fancy decoration or furniture, but it was spacious, clean, and the sofa and chairs were actually a set rather than pieces cobbled together in the hopes they'd look good. On most visits, I'd barely make it through the door of the apartment with my tattered bag of clothes and my toothbrush before my cousin John-John was on me. At night I shared a bed with my cousin in grandma's bedroom. Aunt Mary—who I affectionately called Tina—had the big room in the back.

During the day, John-John and I went everywhere—running neighborhood video game championships, heading into downtown Decatur to catch the MARTA to Walden Middle School in Atlanta to participate in the Bounty Program's production of Romeo & Juliet that John-John and I took part in, and riding our bikes and mopeds on the pothole-free streets of the Misty Waters development.

The grass was cut. They had tennis courts and a clubhouse with a swimming pool. We'd go play tennis and then swim. After, we'd cut over to the field across the way and play ball. One kid would bring a bat; someone else would have a mitt. We got it together somehow, all of us pooling our gear together. If we got tired of playing baseball, we'd go play basketball on the court. During the summer months—when the heavy Georgia heat threatened to melt the Earth itself—we'd spend hours wading and swimming in the pool, playing sharks in the middle. I didn't have a suit of my own. John-John would lend me a pair of shorts and remind me often, half-jokingly, it was bad form I was a better swimmer than he in his own clothes. I loved the feel of the water, pushing through the natural resistance to propel my body forward. I loved it so much, I joined the swim team at the Perry Homes rec center for a couple years.

John-John was taller than I was. Even though I was starting to fill out, my cousin could stand behind me, bend his knees, and be invisible to anyone looking our way. He couldn't understand why our difference in body types didn't translate into more successes for him when challenging me in athletic pursuits. In fact, the only thing he could regularly outperform me in was break-dancing. I could do a nice backspin, but it didn't matter how hard I tried, I could not figure out how to do a windmill. John-John did his best to school me, demonstrating his technique and urging me to keep trying. We spent most of the summer when I was ten practicing. It didn't help. His windmills looked like something out of MTV videos. Mine looked more like a cockroach flipped over on its back struggling to get up than any sort of recognizable dance move. But he had my back and never laughed. Well, he may have laughed a little. I couldn't really blame him.

John-John and I played a lot of video games—Pac-Man and Galaga, mostly. Pac-Man was probably my favorite—actually, Ms. Pac-Man, the fast one. To this day I can't pass a Ms. Pac-Man machine and not hop on for a game. I beat almost every neighborhood kid who challenged me. Man, we'd play forever. Young bucks locked in battle for dominance. It fell to Grandma or Aunt Mary to call a stop every once in a while to make sure we ate lunch and dinner.

* * * * * * * * *

Every day in Misty Waters was like the Fourth of July. Hours of leisure activity and all the good food I could eat. Unlike the residents of Perry Homes, folks in Misty Waters didn't feel compelled to carry concealed firearms in their jackets or tucked into the back of their pants. Music played all the time, drifting out of apartment windows so people outside could dance a little if they felt so inclined. At home when we heard blaring music, it was usually one of Shawty's boys or other drug dealers showing off their hot new vehicles. Kids cleared the streets, heading indoors or to the tree-lined hills of Perry Homes to avoid getting caught in any possible altercation. We were urged not to spend too much time outside without checking in, for risk of getting caught up in something like the series of kidnappings and murders plaguing inner-city families. From 1979-1981, Atlanta native Wayne Williams murdered more than two dozen children and adolescents, striking fear into the hearts of hardened folk who rarely showed fear of anything. Our elders warned us not to go too far past the last set of Misty Waters' units, into the fields and forested area. But besides their vague and quite earnest warnings of what could happen to young children away from streetlights at night, we had free rein to play.

We ruled. And I was the king. Whenever John-John had a beef, he'd come get me to settle the matter. All the other kids had to hear was, I lived in Perry Homes and he was my kin.

"I'm gonna send Rob over," he'd tell boys when they got in his personal space. When I wasn't around, he'd tell them I was coming over on the weekend and they had better leave him alone. John-John had a lot of sudden new best friends as a result of my reputation. I never saw fit to correct their preconceived ideas.

I was a runner. Not a chicken. No, I never fled from a fight. But I preferred running and pushups to pounding other boys' faces in. During the week—after my schoolwork was done—I'd lace up my sneakers and run. And run. And run some more. Like I was trying to match the prodigious cross-country adventures of a slow-witted character from Alabama that would win Tom Hanks an Oscar nod a few years later. I was fit and growing. Often I screamed as I ran, tears flowing down my cheeks while I tried to outrun the demons that plagued me at 579 Clarissa and on the streets of Perry Homes. It was freedom, and strength.

Still, being the boy from Perry Homes had its advantages in Misty Waters. I had respect and no one saw fit to challenge me. There was power there. Pull enough to send the Misty Waters kids running to the convenience store on the corner of Candler Road for some snacks for me or being able to jump to the front of the batting lineup if I wanted. It felt good and right. All my physical activity gave me bulk and muscle, but the badge of Perry Homes gave me respect. I always came home from Misty Waters walking a little taller than I had before my visit.

I also came home with clothes after nearly every weekend. Whatever I needed or wanted, the Huffs provided. John-John loved to look through the upscale catalogues and pick out what he'd like to have—for school, Christmas, his birthday. John-John spent hours poring over the pages. He did it a lot. Sometimes I'd sit and listen to him talk about what the other kids would say when they saw him walking 'round in new designer duds.

"Y'all keep on dreamin'," Aunt Mary shouted good-naturedly from the kitchen.

The fancy-dressed, debonair male models on the pages did seem like dreams. When Aunt Mary took us to the mall in mid-1985, it was my first real foray into the world of high fashion. I did my best to pick outfits—with jeans as their anchor—that would make me look as fine as the men in the catalogues.

We went to Macy's, Rich's, and JC Penney's. I ran my hands back and forth across racks of pressed shirts and crisp denim. I marveled when a salesperson strolled over and asked, "May I help you find anything today?"

I was tempted to grab him by the shirt and scream, "Everything!" But I held my tongue and shook my head. The mall may have been old hand for my cousin, but for me it was a trip to the Riviera. We spent a pocketful of change in the arcade before hitting the food court for some Chick-fil-A chicken, then walked off lunch browsing through the music stores and sporting goods outlets. In the end, I walked away with a pair of designer jeans, a brand-name shirt, and a new pair of leather kicks.

Holidays with Bea, Tina, and John-John were the best. Especially Christmas. Whatever my cousin got for presents, so did I. It was a far cry from the Christmas celebrations I had at home.

Momma Cat—or Momzie if my mother wasn't around—would head over to the Empty Stocking Fund warehouse. Local charities and social services ran programs to help the poor provide for their family during the holidays. Momma Cat got a few vouchers and picked out toys for us—a basketball and hoop for the wall, board games, a Nerf football, or some toy soldiers. Grandma Bea and Aunt Tina seemed to think Christmas was a good occasion to replenish wardrobes. So much so, they often had to buy me a new bag as well to carry my loot home. When John-John's dad was around, which wasn't often, we got cash. Granted, my cousin got more than I did, but I wasn't complaining.

John-John's father was in and out of the picture. When I would show up in Misty Waters and find him there, it was pretty much a guaranteed holiday for us boys even if there wasn't an actual holiday marked on the calendar. He'd call us in to the bedroom and hand out wads of cash. Fifty bucks here, a hundred bucks there—whatever struck his fancy on a particular day. I wanted him to be there every time I paid a visit, but he was often gone months on end, doing time for a variety of petty crimes.

Still, John-John was lucky to have a complete family. And I had the good fortune to be a part of it.

Chapter 8
Stealing Coin

"Get yo' ass in that room and wait on me to come in there. Now," Cat growled from the doorway.

I nearly jumped right out of my skin. I knew her tone. Although I usually heard it when Momma Cat was drunk or high, or both. Sometimes hearing it when she was sober was worse. I knew I was in deep trouble.

Cat found me rummaging in Momzie and Grandpa Ray's closet, like I'd seen her do on more than one occasion, searching for a bit of cash. It had two sections—one side for Momzie, and the other for Grandpa Ray. His side of the closet had less clothing than hers—a mix of button down shirts, slacks, and suit jackets for special occasions. Grandpa Ray was well known for stashing a bit of coin in the pockets of his jackets—a little something tucked away for days when cash was tight.

I came home from school to find the house empty—except for the sound of someone in the bathroom—and figured it was as good a time as ever to grab some change to get me through the week. I hadn't seen the Y.O.U. program coordinator, Kurt, for going on two weeks. Cash was running low waiting for my end-of-the-week reward from Momzie for helping her hustle snacks. I put my schoolbooks down and paused by the bathroom door on my way to Momzie and Grandpa Ray's room. Cat was humming to herself with the shower running. *I should have plenty of time.*

It was easy to find what I needed. There was a wad of singles in the first pocket, but I knew Grandpa Ray counted his money pretty often, so I kept going. All I wanted was a little change, enough to buy some cookies or an ice cream. I had just put my hand into a brown suit jacket and closed my fingers around some change when she spoke.

Cat stood in the doorway with her arms out, hands clasped on the doorframe. She breathed deeply, her chest heaving. Not like she was out of breath, but like she was trying to control herself. Her mouth opened, then closed. She pursed her lips and shook her head slowly.

"Go," she said again after several seconds silence. Momma Cat moved slightly left to let me pass. I skirted past her, wondering what kind of tongue-lashing or beating I might be in for.

I laid down on the contour sofa Tracy and I shared at the time and waited, knowing I'd done wrong. Lamenting the fact I got caught, but knowing I deserved some sort of punishment.

* * * * * * * * *

My eyes flew open at the sound of stomping footsteps. I had just enough time to be in awe over my success in falling asleep before she was on me. I had witnessed Cat beating Tracy pretty bad with a wire hanger once before, and figured if I fell asleep, she might cool down before I woke. She struck, brandishing a white extension cord like a whip. The first blow hit the side of my neck and lower jaw. I barely got my hands up in time to protect my face from the next swing.

Again and again, the blows rained down on me. My forearms and stomach took the worst of it. I rolled off the bed in a bid to escape the pain and turned away from her, only to be rewarded with a series of lashes along my spine and the back of my legs. She grunted, throwing in curse words and insults between swings.

"Cat! Cat, I'm sorry. I ain't gonna do it no mo'." I shouted through the hands covering my face.

"Dumb ... blockhead ...." Momma Cat punctuated each word with a swing of the cord. "I know you ain't gonna do it no mo' 'cause I'm gonna tear yo' roguish ass up."

The extension cord hit me everywhere. I struggled to my feet and looked for a way out. Between Momma Cat's bed and our sleeper sofa, there was only a couple feet of space leading toward the door. Cat—thin and wiry as she was—seemed to grow with her fury, filling the entire room. I abandoned all thought of pleading my case, and focused on bobbing and weaving around the shots. My skin burned. It felt like my body was covered in bee stings—

small pockets of agony sending flashes of pain across my skin and scalding holes into my heart. I stumbled and grabbed the bed for support. Tears flew off my face onto Momma Cat's sheets. I fell to my knees beside the bed. The barrage continued. Eventually I gave up and curled into as small a ball as my growing frame would allow.

Lying there, I was dimly aware of the words coming out of Momma Cat's mouth. "Disrespectin', ungrateful, misbehavin', dishonest ...."

I cried and wished with all my heart we could go back to the days when Cat's physical outbursts were limited to tickle attacks and the occasional slap upside the head.

I couldn't tell how long the beating lasted. It could've been a minute or an hour. The blows became muted, like I'd been given a suit of pillows to muffle the blows. Cat's admonishments continued to rain down from above in an unintelligible string of words I no longer cared to make sense of. My battered arms fell limply to my sides. I rolled over on my back and prayed.

Cat tossed the extension cord to the ground. The end of it whipped around and smacked me upside the head. I turned to watch Cat stomp out and slam the door behind her.

Lying next to a baseball underneath the sleeper was a syringe. I felt new tears burn my eyes. Everything went black.

* * * * * * * * *

I woke up when the door opened and turned my head to find Tracy staring down at me from the doorway. Momma Cat and Momzie's voices trailed from downstairs. I couldn't hear anything beyond their harsh tones. And I didn't care. Tracy snorted and turned away. The door closed and I listened to his heavy-footed jog down the stairs.

I was still lying there with my eyes closed, praying for the guts to move my battered limbs when the door opened and someone else walked in.

"What were you thinking, Robert Lee Yarborough? What were you thinkin'?" Big Larry sat down on the sleeper sofa.

I started to smile at his use of my favorite nickname he'd given me, but a wave of pain crossed my face. His tone was not unkind, so I figured it was safe to gently turn to look up at him. Even through eyes half closed from swelling and prickling with the burn of shame, I saw he took up most of the available space on the bed. Tracy and I barely fit on the thing without fighting each other for enough space to keep our backsides actually in the bed at night, so it wasn't much of a surprise really. I gazed down at Big Larry's feet, wondering if he had any idea there was a syringe lying a few inches behind his right foot. I shrugged in answer to his question.

"You had to know you was gonna be in for trouble if ya got caught. You know that, right?"

"Ye—ye—yessir," I responded, jerking my head side to side to shake off my nerves and keep a steady voice. It didn't work. I dipped my head to hide my embarrassment.

"And you know what you were doin' was stealin', right? And stealin' ain't right."

He waited for me to respond. I didn't dare for fear the tears I held back would escape.

After a few seconds he continued. "If you need something you ask, you hear me? You might get a no, but you might get a yes. That's the proper way, whether you get the result you want or not."

Big Larry told me it was time to get up off the floor and clean myself up. If I wanted to earn a little coin, he had a job I could do on his car. I pulled myself into a sitting position and looked him square in the eye without flinching, even though I really wanted to scream. He nodded and reached out to ruffle my hair before getting up and walking out the door. I looked at the empty doorway and prayed the next time I needed to be taught a lesson, Big Larry would be my teacher.

Chapter 9
Street Corners

The kids were at it again. It wasn't supposed to be this way. I stared out the bus window. Being a part of the Mayor's Youth Leadership Institute (MYLI) was a great opportunity, a chance for intelligent, hardworking kids from across Atlanta to make a difference. With the program we got to interact with city officials, learn how our government worked. It was the best summer job ever. We were also sent into local communities to promote civic literacy and education, to speak with our peers about the importance of being involved in our collective political future.

Riding through the busy streets of Atlanta—passing the museums and universities, the old southern-style architecture of Civil War-era homes interspersed with the modern glass and metal marvels—my chest swelled with pride. But as soon as we approached city housing developments for lower income families, the other kids started taking swipes at me. I wasn't sure why they felt the need to persist after the first couple of times, but it had become routine. I did my best to ignore them, even though I wanted to choke and curse everyone on the bus. Silently, I thanked God for the patience to keep my mouth shut.

"Hey, ain't that where you live, Rob?" one boy shouted across the bus. I looked around, but couldn't tell who said it.

"Wasn't that your momma on the corner?" said another.

The kids around me snickered, even the girls. One of the boys, I couldn't tell which, wondered aloud whether I was a crack baby. His question stung; it rang too true to my circumstances. It wasn't the first time someone tossed the crack baby insult my way. In the third grade, a classmate in Mrs. Heard's class, Chantamika, reveled in repeatedly calling me a crack baby and claimed my mother gave her brothers sexual favors. Her mother was an alcoholic, but Cat was an alcoholic *and* a crack addict, so Chantamika felt she was in a position to put me down. It was excruciating, humiliating—and true. Chantamika's painful jabs only ceased after she and I, along with another 'hood friend Puddin', played house one day. I made sure Chantamika and I played the parts of mom and dad, thinking if I had sex with her, she wouldn't be able to make fun of me anymore. We rolled on the bed for quite some time fooling around and Puddin' was "the child" on the floor. We didn't have sex, but after she stopped making fun of me. My plan worked. But I didn't think the strategy would be effective on the bus.

I glanced around at my MYLI comrades and tossed a half-smile to those who dared catch my eye. I wore a charcoal gray tie and my best shirt—a white button down with pinstripes—I bought with my own money. I was still the most poorly dressed kid on the bus.

If they only knew. My cheeks flushed. To hide my embarrassment, I turned back to the window and waited for the next round of momma jokes. The truth was, it could have been my mother on the last street corner. Most of the time, I didn't know where she was or how she earned money. Heck, she could've been selling candy for all I knew. I would have preferred that to the alternatives I knew took up most of her time. It had been five days since I last saw her—messed up and screaming at Momzie about a sweater she swore was missing. The missing item was hanging in the back of the closet the entire time, but that didn't stop Momma Cat from continuing to raise a ruckus until she stumbled out the door.

I knew even less about Tracy's whereabouts than Cat's. I entered high school just in time to see him drop out. He was ready for the here and now, totally unconcerned by the future. When I asked him why he left, Tracy told me he could make more money out of school than spending half the day sitting in a classroom.

"Only thing worth doin' there is basketball, and I can do that on the street," he said. "You gotta get in where ya fit in 'round here, ya feel me?"

Cat, Momzie, and Big Larry tried to talk him out of it. Big Larry believed he could have a bright career in sports. Momma Cat grabbed him and practically shouted in his face, school learning would help him have a better life than anything in Perry Homes would give him. They nagged ... a lot. A couple times I thought, another beating with a wire hanger might be more effective. All their hours of talking achieved one thing; Tracy rarely came home anymore.

Tracy's departure from school resulted in his automatic removal from one of the first 100 Black Men of Atlanta classes. A group of successful Atlanta businessmen joined forces to help kids get a full education. All participants needed to do was stay with their graduating class throughout high school with a decent grade point average and they would earn a scholarship to attend college. It was one of several great scholastic and athletic programs available. The opportunities enhanced the love I felt for Samuel Howard Archer High School the moment I walked down the steps from the street, across the courtyard, and through the main entrance.

The school's hallways teemed with life, erasing the institutional feel the school's design might have otherwise given. Kids ran back and forth to classes, armloads of books clutched precariously in their hands as they traversed the narrow passageways within the u-shaped building. On Fridays, the entire school turned purple and gold—football players, cheerleaders, and band members wore the school colors with pride.

I was particularly proud to make the football and basketball teams—the two sports I held on to from my days at the Perry Homes rec center. I wanted to be enrolled in the 100 Black Men program as well, but they wouldn't accept additional participants until their inaugural class graduated and headed off to college. It was okay, though.

I could see Tracy's point—lucrative financial opportunities were better outside school. Hanging on the street with other folk from the 'hood meant you didn't have to listen to snide remarks from well-to-do kids on a bus whose parents bought them the latest fashions, gaming consoles, and cars when they turned sixteen.

Most days, me and my little street posse—which included a fine lineup of stand-up guys; Toraino "Reno" Brown, Demarcus "Dee" Hill, "Brother Bill," Lil' Larry and my other cousin Carlos—played basketball or worked on our dance moves. When we were feeling particularly spicy we'd head over to one of the popular teenage dance clubs—Atlanta Live, Fritz or Nightlife—once the sun went to bed for the night. Occasionally, I'd go looking for Tracy with Lil' Larry or Carlos, driving over to the Scottish Inn, Motel 6 or some other shady-looking place on Fulton Industrial Blvd. or Washington Road where it seemed Tracy practically lived full-time.

He had a good setup—a crowd of women at his beck and call, and a steady supply of rock to pawn off on the crackheads hanging out in the parking lots every hour of the day. Sometimes he gave me a few bags to sell for him—as Big Larry, Carlos, and Lil' Larry were doing—and tossed me some cash for my trouble. He cut me a pretty decent deal based on how good business was or how badly he wanted to unload his stock—paying between twenty and thirty dollars for a hundred dollars' worth of rock I peddled. He could afford it.

Chapter 10
"Sprung"

By 'hood standards, she was "a lame," but it didn't matter. From the moment I met her, Commaleta was the one I had to have. She was the kind of girl who took her schooling seriously, wore thick glasses, and played in the Archer High School band. She had a tight apple bottom sheathed in designer jeans, but besides a nice body and pretty face, Commaleta was not necessarily the kind of girl most of the Archer Eagles were looking to hook up with. When they shed their shoulder pads and helmets, Archer Eagles were looking for girls willing to stroke their manhood or at least hang outside the gymnasium doors and make-out. I was certainly no exception, though I kept most of my extra-extracurricular activities away from the prying eyes of the high school gossip machine.

Commaleta was something special—a quiet, intelligent girl with a quick wit, generous spirit, and a kicking body that made my stomach flip-flop every time she walked by. We had Ms. Warrior's English, Ms. Singletary's history, Dr. Rolle's French, and Ms. Lester's algebra classes together. I did my best to saunter in right before the bell and make sure my entrance captured her attention. Anytime she caught my gaze, I felt like I was drowning in those round brown eyes of hers. She was a merciful captor, breaking contact after only a few seconds. Every time she did, it took me a good ten minutes to shake her presence out of my head. At first I was afraid she wasn't interested, but as the weeks passed to months and the eye-mance continued, I knew I had to keep trying. Part of me was a little ticked off; this dorky little flute player wasn't giving up the goods without a fight. I was a man, after all, and shouldn't have to try so hard.

It was okay, though, I could take my time. It wasn't like I didn't have other girls to talk to. Plenty of high school babes were interested in running with a football player. Off school grounds, the pickings were even easier.

Crack was a powerful motivator. I had little interest in smoking it, but I understood the lure of having some in my possession.

It started with Peaches—a woman well into her thirties. With a first-grader at home and another kid in her belly, going out on the streets to get a fix was challenging. "Hey, Rob, you got some blow?" she asked one day out of the blue.

I had known her for years; saw her in front of her apartment watching her daughter play around with her dolls and tricycle. I don't think we ever exchanged more than your basic pleasantries before, but she knew about Tracy's budding business and figured I could hook her up. And I did.

From that day on, all I had to do was swing by Peaches' apartment with a bag or two in my pocket and it was a done deal. She came cheap. A dime bag would do it. Sometimes I would laze back on her couch and make her go down on me; other times, when she was already messed up and sloppy when I got there, I'd mount her.

"You wanna get that kid outta here?" I asked one night a few months into our arrangement. Peaches had her hands and shoulders braced on the couch, knees on the floor as I took her doggie-style. We'd chosen the position because the couch could be noisy and her seven-year-old was upstairs.

I'd looked up to find the girl sitting on the steps and kept right on pumping, waiting for Peaches to respond. I was getting ready to finish.

Peaches screamed at her daughter to go back upstairs.

As soon as I let her go, Peaches reached for the pipe. She didn't even bother to get off the floor or clean herself up. I pulled up my pants and grabbed my jacket on the way out, without so much as a word. Peaches' daughter was sitting on the stairs when I turned around to close the door behind me.

Oh yeah, women were lining up to get them some. I had football and I had crack. I was already a king, even though I was only a sophomore in high school.

* * * * * * * * *

I knew Lawonda wanted me. I'd find her camped out near my locker at least twice a day—far enough away she could play it off like she was getting a drink from the water fountain, but close enough to engage in conversation if she thought she could get away with it. We looked up from the football field most days after school and found her leaning against the school's red brick walls outside the chemistry labs—above and to the right side of the uprights at the parking lot end of the field. She giggled a lot and tossed her hips far and wide when she walked. I didn't pay much attention to her, but occasionally Commaleta was with her, leaning against the wall after band practice ended. She stood out in her purple and gold band uniform. When I knew Commaleta was looking, I played extra hard during those practices.

One day Lawonda said she and Commaleta wanted to talk to me on the phone. I knew my time had come.

"I thought maybe we could go together, you could be my boyfriend. I wanted you to know Commaleta was cool wid'it," Lawonda said.

I pulled the receiver away from my ear and looked at the phone before responding. I had no interest in Lawonda. She had to know it. Why was she pushing the issue? Still, it made me smile a bit. Commaleta had seen how desired I was, if she didn't already know.

"Now looka heh," I said as nicely as I was prepared to be. "I'm trippin' dat bof' o' y'all on da phone at the same time…like y'all tryin' to give an ultimatum or som'n."

"I jus' thought if you knew Commaleta was—"

"Well now if Commaleta said dat I need to heh it from her," I said quickly, cutting her off before she built up steam.

"It really doesn't matter to me," Commaleta interjected bluntly in her squeaky high-pitched, but sweet sounding voice. "It depends on who *you* want to talk to. Which one of us do you like?"

I was profoundly grateful she could not see my blushing cheeks. I chuckled.

Even though she sensed my affection toward Commaleta, Lawonda wasn't prepared to give up right away and was relentless in her attempts to snare me. After a few minutes of monosyllabic responses from me about our upcoming math test, the Eagles' chances for the rest of the season, and a few other inane topics, she finally got off the phone.

"I barely know who you are," Commaleta said, speaking for the first time since Lawonda hung up.

"Well, I know you. You're one of the smartest girls in our class and you play the flute."

"It's a clarinet."

"I know." I savored the silence after. She didn't know who I was? I knew her, and she needed to be put in her place before we went any further.

I talked to her about my love for the gridiron and was only partially surprised to discover a band geek understood anything about football beyond, "Touchdown!"

"Structure is good, it gives you focus," she said after I explained our daily drills. "I'm glad you've got that." Commaleta knew I was from Perry Homes. Her mother, brother, and sister moved into my neighborhood a few months earlier. She was still living with her grandmother in a slightly better section of town, because she didn't want any part of the drugs and crime Perry Homes was famous for.

It took several weeks of talking to convince Commaleta to take me seriously enough to agree to meet after band practice. I fought against her doubts created by nothing I had done personally, but by the questionable reputations of football players everywhere and the Perry Homes residents who had ever broken the law. I was guilty by association. It seemed a little unfair, but it would have been a lie for me to say I wasn't enjoying our conversation. She was smart in ways a ninth grader shouldn't be. Not street smart, no. She was painfully ignorant of what the streets were really like. Commaleta had her sights on the future—the school clubs, grades, and other activities she needed to secure a place at a good college. She gently hinted I should be thankful she'd broken her normal homework and practice routine to spend time talking with me.

"Hope you have yo flute with you tomorrow in class. Might be able to find some use for it," I joked.

"I already told you, Rob, it's a *clar-i-net*."

"I know," I told her and hung up the phone.

I ran upstairs to grab a couple dime bags and stuffed them in my pants—alongside some condoms and my pistol—and headed out to see which girls I could find out on the streets Commaleta despised so much.

Chapter 11
That Package

It was good to be in charge for a change. I grabbed Shanice's head and shoved myself as far into her throat as possible. The other boys around us hooted their delight. I looked over at Reno, who was taking her from behind at the same time. Shanice put her hands up to keep me from plunging back in her mouth.

"Oh no, girl, we're just gettin' started," I said with a laugh. Someone shouted, "Give it to her good Rob!" I winked at the guys.

Shanice agreed to make sure all seven of us came in exchange for a couple dime bags. We were planning to get our money's worth. She could get up and leave any time she wanted—that was the deal. But she'd leave without the crack if she hadn't finished the job.

* * * * * * * * *

I had the afternoon to myself. Homework was done, spring training hadn't begun, and I didn't have a shift at Subway for another two days. I'd started working there a few months prior, the twenty hours or so a week provided a steady official income. Plus I was still selling snacks for Momzie and the extra income allowed me to treat Commaleta to the occasional soda, ice cream cone, or a small gift. She was a good girl. I still hadn't successfully convinced her to go all the way with me, even though we'd been seeing each other for months. In fact, we hadn't gone further than first base since the day I backed her into a corner between the locker room doors and the pathway leading from the back of the school toward the football field. It was her first kiss. I knew because as sweet as she tasted, there was little tongue involved on her part. It was several weeks before we moved beyond and I got the full French treatment. Still, I knew it was only a matter of time, so long as I kept my drug and sexual activities away from her and made sure I continued to be the respectable, loyal, and ambitious person she'd come to know and appreciate.

I spent the few free hours I had between sports practices, school, homework, and Commaleta making sandwiches for hungry folk with a hankering for a footlong. I was working at a sub shop on Howell Mill Road near the Georgia Institute of Technology—better known as Georgia Tech. Meeting a variety of professors, students, and administrators—even if only for brief encounters—was kind of cool. I discovered most of them talked like they were reading from textbooks, rather than the slang I normally heard. I'd been exposed to people "talkin' proper" on television, radio programs, through teachers at school and conversation with Commaleta, but not with this much regularity. The more sandwich orders I processed, the more I realized it was people inside the 'hood who sounded different from the rest of the city's residents. But it wasn't just the way they talked; it was also what they talked about. That was the biggest difference between the college crowd and my neighborhood acquaintances. I had a front row seat to watch, listen, and learn.

It became a form of extra homework, studying the way these people conducted themselves. Mothers gently coaxed their young ones along the counter and made sure they got plenty of vegetables on their sandwiches during pit stops on their way to gymnastics practice or a dance recital. Businessmen in suits opened briefcases full of documents to work on while they ate. College-age kids were full of talk about philosophy and politics—how Nietzsche's "God is dead" adage applied as easily to Cold War-era circumstances as it did to the world that existed when it was first expressed. I had to look up Nietzsche to figure out why they talked about him so much. I envied them, the life experience they were gathering, and I desperately wanted to be a part of their world.

Most of the customers from the college were polite, but distant. It was clear by their demeanor that ordering food was their only interest in the acne-plagued teenager behind the counter. Others were downright rude, barking their food orders like I was simpleminded and couldn't tell the difference between an olive and tomato. At fifteen, I was the restaurant's youngest employee. The rest of the staff—down to the seventeen-year-old part-timer with worse acne than mine—felt entitled to boss me around. I mopped a lot of floors and stocked a lot of condiments.

Still, it was better than sitting around at home listening to nonstop laments about Tracy. Momzie, Grandpa Ray, and Big Larry seemed to think it necessary to remind me what a mistake he was making being out of school, like I might be contemplating the same move. Venturing into the kitchen to get a drink was a risky maneuver. Momzie started haranguing me over pots of food about what I was planning to do to help them get Tracy back in school. I reminded her occasionally I was the younger sibling and Tracy was unlikely to listen to me. It's not smart to argue with a woman who just pulled gizzards out of a bird with the precision of a surgeon, though.

Tracy came back to school after the holidays—more for Momzie and Momma Cat's sake than his own, I think. Once the basketball season ended, his attendance dropped rapidly. It was obvious he was done with school for good. I dreaded the moment Momzie, Grandpa Ray, Momma Cat, and Big Larry found out. I cursed him more than once for not telling them. As soon as they discovered his departure, it somehow became my responsibility to convince him he was wrong.

* * * * * * * * *

I moved to switch places with Reno and made sure to put on a new condom. Shanice had started to tire about ten minutes in and I was pretty sure her teeth nicked the one I was wearing. It was a wonder how she planned to get through the other five guys, but I honestly didn't care. Running a seven-man train was fun. Besides, she asked for it.

Shanice reveled in driving all us "little boys" crazy a few years back—flashing her body, but refusing to give it up to anyone. Until she started basing out. Her slide down the black rock came at a cost for good ol'e Shanice. She was still good looking, but she wasn't nearly as put together as once before. Her clothes were stained and well worn, her face empty of makeup—sure signs she spent what little money she had elsewhere. She'd had a kid or three along the way, too, even though she was only a couple years older than me and my homeboys. When she'd approached me and asked tentatively about a deal, I knew I could have anything I wanted from her. The sparkle in her eyes was replaced by a wild-eyed glare belying her single-minded purpose—more crack. Hell, I probably could've gotten into her for a single dime bag. But I was feeling generous and didn't want to insult her. Now there she was—jeans pulled to her ankles, down on her knees in dried spit, piss, and God knew what else—in an alleyway full of teenagers stroking themselves and waiting impatiently for a turn.

I was done letting women or anyone get the better of me. I was in charge. It hadn't always been this way. One of the girls I'd had on call for sex tried to pull one over on me. Ronda told me she was nineteen. One day when she was over at 579 Clarissa, I went in her pocketbook and grabbed her ID—Ronda was only twelve. She got mad when she saw me with her ID and slapped me hard on the back. I reacted without thinking and slapped Ronda upside the head. She fell back on the bed and started sobbing. By the time she stopped crying and we walked to the bus stop, she had talked me into continuing our trysts.

A couple months later, Ronda was pregnant and I had crabs. Reno gave me some shampoo and I called to confront her. She said the crabs were from using a washcloth to clean up at a friend's house. I didn't believe her; told her I had no respect left for her and wanted to end it. When Ronda originally told me about the pregnancy, I contemplated dropping out of school to support her and the baby. Now with obvious lies about the crabs, I wasn't prepared to trust her on anything. If she was pregnant, I doubted it was mine. I hung up the phone. A few minutes later, her friend called back and claimed Ronda was jumping on her stomach, trying to kill the baby. I didn't believe a word of it.

Being a leader meant being smart. Even though a couple of the boys were watching me fumble to change condoms with goofy sex-crazed grins on their faces, I knew what I was doing. Plenty of people in the 'hood had been getting *that package*—and it wasn't the postal service doing the delivering. Like most across the country, folks in Perry Homes initially disregarded reports of the "gay disease" sweeping through homosexual communities in places like San Francisco and New York. It didn't take long before

HIV/AIDS moved into our area. A few of Momma Cat's party friends contracted it—two had already died. On more than one occasion, Big Larry and Momzie urged Momma Cat to take care. Most people knew enough to watch out for the druggies—especially the ones doing smack and sharing needles. When word began to spread that the infected could pass it on during sex too, I went to Ike's market to buy a pocketful of condoms, or raided the seemingly endless supply in Big Larry's dresser, to keep with me at all times.

I banged Shanice from behind not looking at her, with my face turned toward the rest of the boys leaning against the wall. They needed to know who was in charge of this gathering and I wanted them looking me in the eye as I displayed my dominance. It would take a while with all these people watching. Nevertheless, to keep myself from finishing too quickly, I thought about other things—the pot of collard greens I'd seen simmering on the stove before I left 579 Clarissa, Tracy's indecision over whether to get another tattoo or a set of grillz for his front teeth, Big Larry's new orange shirt. I wasn't sure it was a good color for him when he'd danced by me the night before on his way out for a date.

I almost fell out of Shanice when an image of Momma Cat in one of her pretty dresses—the blue one—popped into my head. I didn't know where she was, or what she was doing, but I hoped it wasn't something like what I was doing. I pushed the thought out of my head and got back to work. Didn't want the boys to see any sign of weakness.

It was another ten minutes before I stepped back from the plate, removed the cock sock, and wiped my hands clean on the back of Shanice's shirt. "Handle yo' bih'ness fellas," I told the others and headed out the alleyway buckling my belt. Reno fell in step beside me. Behind us came the unmistakable sounds of the other guys jostling for position.

In the end all seven of us came in that alleyway—me, Reno, Mike, Monte, Duck, Derrick and Reggie. A few months later I heard on the street, Shanice had gotten that package.

Chapter 12
Forty Kills

Eight balls were my thing. Enough dope to make some quick money, but not a big enough stash to make me a target for other dealers or junkies. Sometimes Shawty offered two-for-one deals on his dime bags. On the weeks when I had a lot of hours at work, football practice, and a lot of schoolwork, it was a handy way to save time and turn a quick profit. But most of the time I bought eight balls—carving them up using the skills I gleaned from watching Big Larry and Tracy and putting the pieces into small baggies. I cut up mostly dime bags. Nickels were penny pinching, not worth my time. I wanted to more than double my initial investment. It was easy money.

On the surface, all anybody needed to know was I peddled chips, cookies, and chocolate snacks to my schoolmates. I liked it that way because I didn't want to get caught. Selling crack would get me kicked off the football team and probably land me in juvie or the local detention center, like Tracy and so many others on at least one occasion. I wanted the money, but I sure didn't want any official kind of trouble, so I had to play it smart.

I did my business quickly and efficiently, staying off the streets as much as possible. It was habit to hand off a bit of my product to Reno, or my boys Mookie and Big Dave, after school or on the way to a shift making subs, so I had cash coming in while cutting my risks. My co-conspirators were too busy on the street to lend a hand serving Momzie's plates or sell chips. They were happy for the chance to make a little extra something. I had little interest in the brawls and other mischief unfolding on street corners in Perry Homes. For the most part, I stayed at home if I wasn't working. It was a pretty ideal setup.

Tracy embraced "the life," abandoning the family dramas of

579 Clarissa to find fortune alongside his thug friends. Initially, he was only gone on weekends, but his absences quickly turned full-time. He was living on-and-off at the various hotel-motels on Fulton Industrial and Washington, so he could mess with whatever he wanted—drugs, women, drinking, silk outfits, alligator shoes, fast cars.

I understood the attraction. As I drove over toward Fulton Industrial to find Tracy and talk to him about Momma Cat, I was angry. A child shouldn't have to worry about their parent. Not that way. I turned to God for comfort but I had to work for the result I wanted. The weather seemed to be cooperating, at least, and I kept myself amused during stops by watching the cool late autumn breeze move through the trees. Tracy wouldn't be too hard to find. If he wasn't at the hotels or on the street corner dealing, he would be in one of the strip clubs over on Marietta, Bankhead, or Stewart Streets. He was pretty partial to Body Tap and Blue Flame.

It wasn't Cat's cussing, grabbing, or yelling giving me grief. Hell, we were all used to the headaches Momma Cat raised when she was in a mood to fight. I was even used to her disappearing acts. She had pretty much moved out. We weren't sure where, and whenever we asked, she'd simply say she had a place to lay her head. But the last time she'd come home to 579 Clarissa, a couple days before, she'd dissolved into tears in the midst of a fierce cussing fit after opening a cupboard to get a glass and a cockroach came tumbling out. Cockroaches were nothing new. We all knew any time you went down into the kitchen after sundown, you best be prepared for a massive cascade of creepy-crawlies when you opened the cupboards. But she stood there, glass in hand, wide-eyed with a tear running down her bony cheek, like she just didn't know what to do. I walked across the kitchen to see if she was okay. She shrugged away, said, "Muthafucka," and walked out of the house with the glass still in her hand. I didn't know if she threw the parting epithet at me or the cockroach. I hadn't seen her since.

I figured Tracy was older, knew more about the world she was living in, and might have something to say about her strange behavior. He'd taken to giving Momma Cat crack to smoke on occasion, so she might actually listen to him. If we could find her. Aunt Brenda, Big Larry, and Momzie had tried to steer Cat toward staying at home more, and maybe finding a steady job. Momma

Cat didn't seem to want any part of it. Half the time—the occasions when she wasn't messed up—she didn't even bother to get heated about their advice like she had so many times in the past. "It's my life, I'm livin' in," she'd tell them and then refuse to participate in the conversation any further.

Tracy was all about his street friends. He gave them time, money, or drink before he'd give anything to his family. After I found him in one of the motel parking lots with a couple of his buddies, the only thing that seemed to matter to him when we started talking was his image.

"What you see is what you get, so you better get it. I'm gonna make me that money, bro. You can belie'dat. Cat's doin' her thing and there ain't no wrong in that. It is what it is."

Tracy talked about getting a sweet ride—a Cadillac, like all the dope boys wanted. Or a big body Bonneville. Or a Cutlass. "Imma get dat bitch tricked out wit' da goddamned candy apple red paint and peanut butter guts on dey ass."

I guess I half expected it, but couldn't keep the disappointment off my face when he went on about cars and clothes instead of our mother.

"Don't be lookin' at me like 'dat, school boy." He poked a finger into my chest. "I'll talk to ya anytime you want, 'cause lawd knows you don't do much talkin' yo'self, but you gonna know imma keep it real. Ain't no fancy talk up in 'ere.

"Jus' keep on doin' what you doin' bro. Go and get yours. Keep on doin' what you do. Ya gonna be a'right, ya gonna be successful … take it to another level," he said gently after sending his buds away with a nod. "You already ready, fool. I knows it even if you don't. Don' you worry 'bout Momma Cat no mo'."

His sudden candor surprised me. I was grateful for his faith in me, and shocked he chose to express it. Trying to use the street to my advantage, same as he was; he knew I was having my share of scraps. Mostly street brawls, fist-on-fist, but several times people had pulled knives or guns. Only a fool would walk the streets of Perry Homes without something to back them up.

I looked at Tracy's face, trying to read his expression. He was smiling, but there was something in his eyes. It felt like his plea for me to succeed was his way of keeping his lost dreams for a different, easier life alive. For a brief moment, I thought maybe I didn't know him at all. I wondered if he knew how close I'd come to using my gun recently.

* * * * * * * * *

Not having a car of my own, I needed to borrow my cousin Carlos' Cutlass to pick up a friend I was hooking up with. My plan was to stay out all night, so I couldn't ask Momzie or Big Larry for their cars. It would have raised too many questions.

I told Alicia I would wait for her in the parking lot of the Church's Chicken restaurant near her neighborhood. I didn't want to drive to her place to get her and potentially spark any talk about what we might be doing, or step into an ambush. I'd only met her once before. We'd talked on the phone a couple times—agreed to hook up and have sex—but it didn't mean I could trust her. I might be eager, but I wasn't stupid. Commaleta still wasn't giving up the goods, so I crafted an on again, off again relationship with her, and did what I pleased with other girls. It didn't mean I had to advertise what I was getting into, though.

It wasn't like I hadn't tried to be primarily with the one girl in my life I had strong feelings for. A month before, I'd taken Commaleta out for dinner and a movie, and then to a nice hotel for the night. Commaleta's mother kept a close eye on her daughter and normally restricted her activities. She also trusted her because of a long track record of good grades, good behavior. When Commaleta concocted a cover story, spending the night with a cousin, her mother believed it. The hotel wasn't anything too fancy, your average sort of thirty-nine-ninety-five a night type deal—but it was clean and the room had a television in it. It became quickly apparent we had different intentions in mind. At first I thought she was being a tease. The reality was, Commaleta was still a virgin. She was only interested in cuddling for the night. I got a little aggressive, grinding against her and trying to pull her underwear off, even as she asked what I was doing and resisted. We were kissing just fine, so I figured she needed a little more time to get ready. I thought I needed to keep up the effort and she'd let me have it. In the end, the excitement made me climax on her thigh.

After, I got hungry and dressed to go to the store. I placed my

.38 on the nightstand and told Commaleta, if anyone came through the door but me, she should start blasting. She looked at me like she didn't know me.

"Are you kidding me? I ain't gonna shoot nobody," she said softly, shaking her head. "And why are you carrying a gun?"

Her question shook me a bit. She was unaware of my drug dealing and could not fully grasp my need to carry at all times. I responded quickly, as naturally as possible, "You know these fools on the streets'll try you. I have to be ready to protect my own."

"Well, I don't like the idea of you carrying. Guns are too dangerous, Rob. They cause more trouble than they solve."

I understood her concern, but dismissed it. Being in my line of work was not for the faint of heart. Survival came at a price too enormous for her to calculate. Commaleta crawled into bed and pulled the sheets up to her chin. I knew she had bought my explanation and felt no need to cross-examine me. But the look in her eyes told me she was displeased with my decision.

Looking down at her, I knew she was telling the truth. There was no way this girl, with a cherub's face and a voice like melting butter sliding down the sides of a hot baked potato, would ever pull a trigger. Guns, drugs ... it wasn't her world, and never would be. Even if it was the environment in which she was forced to survive.

Women are funny, I thought and looked through the Church's Chicken window to the diners inside. A man and woman were leaving the restaurant. The warbling tones of Whitney Houston's megahit about never-ending love drifted into the parking lot. I snorted and leaned over to hit the radio.

As I sat up from changing the radio station, movement to my left caught my attention. A man—obviously a junkie—stood not too far away. When you've been around enough people strung out on any number of crazy mixes of drugs and alcohol, you learn how to tell the difference between an occasional partier and bona fide addict. He stared at me with wide eyes. I could practically hear him thinking, *A young guy sitting in a parking lot by himself after sundown is easy prey. I can get the jump on him.*

He lumbered forward, taking no real care to mask his intentions. He stared at me, raising his eyebrows and jerking his head at me every few seconds, issuing a silent challenge.

I answered by pulling my .38 out of my jacket pocket and holding it in plain view. I'd bought the gun a few months back from Lamont, a Perry Homes businessman. "That thing's got forty kills on it," he'd told me when I held it for the first time and gave it a pre-purchase once-over. I gave him forty bucks for it, one for each death. It was a just deal.

The junkie stopped, looked at the gun, then back at my face. My shoulders tensed. I waited for him to lunge. Watched for tells in his eyes, hoping to catch a movement to help me get the jump on him.

He smiled and gave me a lopsided half-grin before turning to shuffle away, his hands in the pockets of his tattered jeans. The guy had no clue he was about to become kill number forty-one. I realized I had seriously been ready to shoot him and shrugged. It wasn't the first time I'd been ready to pull the trigger. When Reno called on me for help a couple weeks prior to this incident, I responded without question.

Some punk had aimed the red beam of his gun on Reno's brother-in-law's chest. I ran to get the pump—Big Larry's shotgun—and raced to the car. Halfway to Reno's, I realized I was wearing only shorts and a pair of boots. I was ready to do whatever necessary to help Reno get retaliation. In the end we were lucky nobody got shot—by the time I arrived, the punk was long gone.

When Alicia showed up, my mind was on anything except sex. But the moment I saw her spandex leopard outfit and high heels, I was good and ready for some heart-pounding, mind-numbing intercourse. The kind that left you so exhausted, you couldn't think of anything but lying in bed after. She didn't disappoint. We went a few times during the night and it was good. I didn't do any cuddling between rounds. I only cuddled with Commaleta.

The next morning when I took her home, we got pulled over because I was speeding. Fortunately, the cop chose not to search the car or he would've found the unlicensed weapon, and probably the sacks of crack I had in my pocket when he pulled me out of the car.

I was extremely lucky; the weapon that had saved my life the night before hadn't cost me the rest of it at a routine traffic stop.

Chapter 13
When the Streets Invade

The household was in an uproar. Momzie tucked herself into a recliner, a throw blanket over her knees, cradling a hot cup of something and staring at the floor. My baby cousin Tiffany—who was just approaching her eighth month—whined and fussed in her mother's arms. Big Larry stomped back and forth across the small living room. He was cursing in ways generally not tolerated in Momzie's company. I wasn't sure what was going on. I'd walked in the door to find the living room crowded with family members.

"Momzie?"

My grandma slowly shook her head.

Big Larry answered.

"Mutherfuckers came righ'in the house, man. Right in, an' put guns to everybody's heads!"

Big Larry stomped to the back door and wrenched it open. I dropped down next to Momzie's recliner, the muscles in my back and neck tense as I processed what he said. I still didn't know exactly what was going on, but I knew he'd fill me in. *What I do know is, I'm tired of mutherfuckers fucking with me and my family. And I know what to do.* There had been a couple occasions over the last few months when I'd stepped forward to defend what was mine and protect the people I loved.

* * * * * * * * *

I was already in a pretty bad mood when Pierre—who was from France—turned and told me to grab condiment refills, talking real slow, like he thought I didn't understand English or didn't know how to run the shop. He was older than me and he'd been an employee at Subway just a couple months. I wasn't thrilled but thought, "Okay, I'll do it for a moment." I was in my second of three years working at that particular location. And I liked it there.

As soon as I was done, he ordered me to do another task. "Go and get the veggies." And after that, yet another. "Get some more sliced meats. Can't you see what we need on the line?"

I had enough. "Man, you need to chill out on that, bro. I don' know who you think you talkin' to."

"I'm talking to you," he answered with his silly little French accent.

"What, you think I started working here yesterday? You don't need to be telling me what to do, man."

I went for my bag and pulled my pistol out, making a point of walking back and forth near him with it in my hand. "You just see what happens you keep talkin' that shit," I muttered loud enough for him to hear. "Tired of dumb muthafuckers tellin' me what to do. You betta' take that shit back to France or sum-goddamned-where befo' yo' ass get dealt wit' up in heh."

Out of the corner of my eye, I saw a group of people walking up to the door. I stuffed the pistol into my apron, the butt clearly visible, and stepped up to the line. Frenchie beat a hasty retreat to the backroom and didn't come back for a while.

"What'cho wan'?" I snarled at the first guy who walked in. He was wearing glasses and looked about college aged.

"Can I get a turkey sub on white?"

"Can I get a turkey sub? This is a sandwich shop ain't it, fuckin' dummy," I murmured, reaching to grab the bread.

When I turned back around I caught him staring at the butt of the gun. "You want this all the way?"

"Uh, what do you think I should have?"

He kept it cool through the transaction. He didn't even flinch when I proclaimed, "Mutherfucker's jus' lucky I don't pop him one in the ass," while stacking lettuce and tomatoes on top of the meat. I don't know whether the customer got the sandwich he wanted or the one I chose for him, but he made it out alive. Pierre didn't say a word to me after.

I almost wished he had. This was the third time I'd pulled out my gun and failed to use it.

A couple months before, Tracy barged through the door of 579 Clarissa in a rage. A guy we knew from the 'hood had taken the parking spot in front of our apartment and refused to move when Tracy asked. Tracy, Lil' Larry, and I went out to confront him—carrying a .380, 9mm, and .38, respectively. We stood in a line right outside the door. Behind us, Brenda and Grandpa Ray stood ready with small firearms of their own. The man still refused. His cousin, who was less inebriated than he was, did his best to diffuse the situation. While he talked, I made mental preparations to take a shot and make an escape through the trees and pathways of Perry Homes. I wanted to be the one to do it. I was the youngest; I wanted to shine. Instead, the cousin assured us they would vacate the parking spot.

* * * * * * * * *

"We was jus' sittin' there. Me and Tiffany and Jovonda, eatin' us some buffalo wings on the bed, when they came in," Big Larry explained.

There had been three intruders. Momzie let them in when they said they were Larry's friends. Two headed upstairs. The third remained in the living room with a pistol aimed at Momzie and baby Tiffany's mom.

They walked into Big Larry's room and asked for two bags. When Larry asked him what the heck he was talking about, one of them pulled out an Uzi. "You know what dis is, nigga, you know what it mean, and goddammit, I want it. Now you git up, nigga, and show me where it's at."

"I don'know who sent you here, but there's kids in the house, man. What the fuck is you doin'?" Larry admitted after, his anger made it hard to think his way out of the situation. "Y'all done come in the wrong house, I tell ya that, man."

The thug with the gun hit Big Larry on the side of the head and demanded his entire marijuana stash and all the cash Larry had. The second guy made a grab for the baby. But as soon as they recovered the reefer and coin from a sock in Larry's drawer, they wanted more—his stock of cocaine. Big Larry told them it was in a shoe under his bed. He realized it was an inside job, even though those particular thugs weren't Perry Homes residents.

They backed Big Larry down the stairs with the Uzi trained on him and shoved him onto the couch. Jovonda made a bold move to break free and successfully sprinted out the back door. Nobody knew what the thugs intended to do—roll the family for other valuables or shoot people. But the moment Jovonda escaped, they backed off and made a break for the front door with my uncle screaming after them.

"Only a couple people knows I started dealing blow in the last week, so they could only get that from three or fou' people … an' I know who it was. They gonna pay," Larry promised.

I sat there marveling at how far removed this situation was from the loves in my life—football and Commaleta—and how intertwined the two had become for me. We had our routines. On practice days, Commaleta waited for me after band practice until we were done—maybe give me some hugs and kisses when I came back out of the locker room all cleaned up. Game days, we'd head over to Ms. Betty's apartment and grab a juicy cheeseburger before heading back to school, pumped for the challenge and lights that powered our Friday nights. Some weeks, after the game was over and my girl back at home, I'd jog out of Perry Homes and head back to school. Folks from the neighborhood thought I was crazy, running down the streets in the dark at midnight or later for no good reason they knew of. Aside from small children playing, if you saw people running in Perry Homes it was usually because they were in danger.

Sitting there on the slope on the side of the field where the bleachers were, I could look across the gridiron to the outlines of the trees beyond. Every few minutes, I'd get up and run round the track circling the field, or up and down the hill, before sitting down again. It was my chance to get away from the violence in Perry Homes. It gave me time to talk quietly with God about the things I wanted to do, to focus and pray on how I worked for success on the field and in school. My family didn't seem to think my running was quite as crazy as my bathroom mirror screaming sessions, so they left me to it without question.

My personal frustrations would always take second place behind my determination to protect my family. It was God first, family second, and everything else after. That's what Big Larry tried to teach me on so many occasions. He was right. I would do what was needed—help Big Larry hunt the criminals who invaded our home and get us some proper justice.

"Naw, Robert Lee Yarborough, this bizness ain't for you." Big Larry stopped his preparations to walk over and put his hand on my shoulder. "Your job is those books, that's where you need to be."

I knew he meant it. Big Larry had gathered us boys—me, Tracy, Lil' Larry, and Carlos—more than once and told the rest of them to keep their street messes away from me. When we'd had word on a previous occasion about someone looking to shoot Lil' Larry over a woman, Big Larry made me stay inside while he and his sons went outside with a rifle and pistols to take care of it. He wouldn't interfere with me dabbling in street business so long as I kept my nose clean, but the less involved I was, the better. In fact, he'd said it so many times I knew what was going to come out of his mouth before he started to speak again.

"You just in the wrong place, Rob. You don' need to be tryin' to fit in with everybody else … you jus' keep workin' on up outta here. We'll handle this." He grabbed his shotgun, camouflage jacket, and slipped a pistol into his pocket.

I found it difficult to concentrate on my homework as Big Larry, Carlos, and Lil' Larry went off to hunt the guys down. But I did what I was told. I kept Momzie company in the living room, both of us crouched on the floor in case something went wrong and they came back looking for blood. I prayed to God to bring my family members back home safe and sound.

After a home invasion of their own and a shakedown for the guy Big Larry suspected had helped set up the robbery, they discovered the intruders' names and where they hung out, but Big Larry and Lil' Larry never found them. We later heard the guys who invaded our home and held the family at gunpoint had ended up in prison. On their way back from Perry Homes, their weapons and the drugs they'd stolen were discovered during a routine traffic stop. It wasn't exactly justice the way Big Larry sought and we all wanted, but it would do.

Chapter 14
Package Delivered

I gripped the wheel so tight, it about snapped in two. I knew from Momma Cat's demeanor that something was up. She'd never asked me to drive her home before. For well over a year, nobody in the family aside from Big Larry knew exactly where she was living.

Why now? I wondered and stole a glance at her. Her face was partly obscured by shadow, only the left side clearly visible in the circle of light from the street lamp on the other side of the road. *It should be brighter out here*, I noted, but the rest of the street lamps were broken.

We were sitting in Momzie's tan Cadillac Cimarron. I loved that car. The leather interior, air conditioning, and power mirrors were cool, but the front of the car was my favorite part. Cimarrons had an extended hood which made up nearly a third of the overall body. It stretched out in front of me while I drove, telling everyone it was time to get outta my way, like a bodyguard leading a star quarterback through a crowd of fans.

Cat had a small spot in a rooming house on McDaniel Street— the kind of place where residents shared a common shower and little else. No one would ask Momma Cat questions about her comings and goings there. I knew she preferred it that way.

While I waited for her to speak, I looked the place over. It was a large colonial style house, covered in indigo paint that was chipped and peeling off in large strips. Momma Cat's room was upstairs, the corner room on the second floor in the back. About the only good thing I saw about the rooming house was the rooms on the second floor didn't have bars on the windows.

"Robert, I got something to tell ya." Cat paused briefly between each word, like she was picking them with excruciating care. She didn't look at me, just stared straight ahead. I waited for her to continue.

"You know I got AIDS, don't'cha?" she said in a rush and snickered. "Doctor says I got AIDS."

From her tone, one would've thought she was delivering the punch line to a joke. For a few seconds I dared to hope she was. But I watched her rapidly clasping and unclasping her hands with uncontrollable nervousness and knew there was nothing to laugh about.

"You, uh, wanna see the papers or somethin'? I got 'em in one of my pockets heh." She pulled the papers out after a little digging. Momma Cat giggled, took my hand off the steering wheel, and shoved a wad of documents into my unwilling hand.

"I knew for a while now. Was a'right at first, but now I'm not feeling so good a lot of times an' I thought I better tell ya," she continued. "I'm jus' getting sicker and sicker now."

I stared at her openmouthed, the wad of documents crumpled in my hands. Light reflected off a thin line down the side of her face. Momma Cat was crying.

I choked out a handful of words, asking her how she'd contracted AIDS and was taken aback when she responded.

"I was raped." She told me two men had put a knife to her throat and forced her into a car to have their way with her.

It was obvious from the way she hid her face after catching my eye, she knew I could tell she was lying. The worst part was, it was quite possible the sexual assault did occur, but it was far more likely she'd contracted AIDS as the result of years of careless lifestyle choices. She didn't seem willing to take any responsibility for what was happening to her, though.

"Ain't no big deal," I whispered, turning my head to look out the window. Tears fell freely down my cheeks.

Plenty of people were getting that package—if you believed the street—walking 'round the 'hood with the disease coursing through their veins like it was nothing. Heck, I heard stories practically every other day about someone taking delivery of the package. Although we all knew HIV/AIDS would lead to death, it was too remote a reality for most of us in the 'hood to really process. Life in Perry Homes was about making it through today and hoping to make it to tomorrow. What was the point of worrying about a disease killing you a few months or years down the road when a single gunshot at any moment could end your existence?

But this is Cat. All her joking and messing around about having AIDS couldn't erase the terrifying reality. I thought about the seventh-grade project I'd done on AIDS, how the disease was contracted and how it attacked a body once inside. AIDS was a death sentence. *How long have you known Cat?* My throat constricted and the pieces of Momzie's chicken I had for dinner felt like they were strutting 'round my stomach, trying to put themselves back together again. I swallowed hard to control myself and turned in my seat to face Cat.

"Okay, so what's next?" My voice was harsher than I'd intended.

Momma Cat stole a glance at me. I rushed on, not giving her a chance to respond. "Okay, you got AIDS. You're still sitting here, still behaving the way you always do, so it can't be all that. It doesn't change anything, nothing's different."

"Okay then," she answered quietly. I sat there glaring at her. She opened her mouth to speak and closed it again.

A battle raged inside me, torn between anger and fear as I waited for her to find words. I was glad I stopped dealing crack. I silently thanked God again for my crack addicted uncle Johnny Ray—Cat and Larry's brother—stealing my stash out of the bedroom a couple of months before. He had done me a powerful favor. Once I discovered the dope was missing, I decided I didn't want to pour any more of my money into the drug business. I would earn what I could selling snacks and working at the restaurant. I was done taking stupid risks.

"We good then?"

I paused before answering. It wasn't what I had expected her to say. Then it hit me. Her words went beyond the here and now, beyond the troubling discussion unfolding in the front seats of Momzie's Cadillac. After everything that had happened, even in the face of approaching doom, Cat was unable to express herself meaningfully in the quest for forgiveness. She couldn't make herself apologize for the hell she'd put me through, and acknowledged the failures she committed during her tenure as a mother the only way she knew how—by avoiding them. It made me angry and sad. I knew her intentions were sincere; it was the best she could do.

"Yeah. Yeah, we good," I assured her.

I leaned over to stop her when she went to grab the door handle, and only let her leave the car after I'd given her a strong hug. It was one of the last times I would have the chance.

It hit me again on the way home, she never did tell me, honestly, how she contracted HIV/AIDS. Chances were she didn't even know. Between all the sex she'd had and whatever drugs she'd done, it was a toss-up. A lot of her friends were dying of AIDS-related complications. I should have guessed something was wrong when a nurse from the community health services place started showing up at 579 Clarissa looking for Momma Cat. She brought medicine, a cocktail of pills to try and fight off the disease. On the rare occasion Momma Cat was in the apartment when the nurse came, she'd pretend she wasn't there. Cat kept saying she didn't need to take twenty pills a day. It wore on her, she'd said. I wondered if it was the reason she spent progressively less and less time visiting us over the last year.

Her revelation raised a lot of questions I doubted I'd ever know the answers to. I always prayed for Momma Cat, but that night before bed, I asked God to ease her pain and mine. If He couldn't do both, I'd keep mine as long as she could find some peace.

Chapter 15
Beneath the Sheets

We had the perfect plan. I was going to bring Lashaune home with me for a round and I'd share the goods with Lil' Larry. She was good to go, one of my go-to girls—we'd had sex on several occasions before. All Lil' Larry had to do was watch out the window and jump in the closet when he saw us coming up the walk.

"Even though it's dark, I'm going to flip her up over on her stomach, so you don't have to worry about her seeing you or nothing. All you have to do is hop in when I tell ya," I instructed him. When he was done, Lil' Larry just had to slip back into the closet and I would take Lashaune home, none the wiser.

"A'right yeah. Yeah I can do'dat," he said quickly. I could tell by the way he kept licking his lips and shifting weight from one foot to the other while I told him the plan, he was eager for his share.

I smiled and went out to grab Lashaune off the street. We shared everything at 579 Clarissa—I guess because we didn't have all that much to begin with and family has to stick together. The only thing I wasn't too excited to share were shoes after all the years living with Tracy's athletes' foot. But jackets, shirts, cars, girls? No problem. Heck, Carlos had even seen fit to borrow my driver's license a few weeks back without asking. I can't say I would have minded if he asked.

Lashaune followed me upstairs, careful not to attract Momzie or Grandpa Ray's attention. They were in their room, lying down to relax and watch some television. As soon as I shut the bedroom door behind us, we got straight to business.

A few minutes in, I told her I didn't want to come in the missionary position and flipped her over. Just as I was about to reach my conclusion, I pulled out and told her I wanted to adjust my position.

With the condom still on, I backed in to the closet. I didn't have to worry about making any noise—it didn't have a door for me to run into. Lil' Larry brushed past me on his way out.

I heard him get to work, grunting like he was trying to mimic my voice. So far the plan was working like a charm.

Less than a minute later, Lashaune hollered.

"Who is this?"

"It's Rob ... Robert," Lil' Larry said, dropping his voice down low like mine.

"Lil' Larry? Is that—"

"What you talking 'bout?" Lil' Larry cut her off. It was a mistake. The more he spoke, the more he gave Lashaune the confirmation she needed.

"Get your black ass up off me! What the hell kind of fucked up shit you trying to pull here?"

Lil' Larry backed up and pulled my bed sheet around his neck, like he was some new kind of caped super hero—Naked Man! I emerged from the closet with a flock of butterflies attacking the inside of my stomach. Lashaune bowed her head into her hands in apparent embarrassment. With a speed I didn't know he had, Lil' Larry sprinted out of the room. Lashuane looked up in shock. We were silent—me looking at her and then out the window, she stared at the floor. The sounds of Lil' Larry pounding down the stairs faded. Lashaune covered her face again and kept silent.

The sound of my pulse echoed in my ears. *I jus' gotta get the fuck up outta here and make me an exit.* I started to tiptoe past Lashaune, not intending to say a word.

"Robert?" she called after me.

I squared my shoulders and padded down the stairs to stand opposite Lil' Larry at the bottom. As I waited for him to speak, I realized I didn't have a stitch of clothing on my body.

"She gonna say she was raped, cuz. What we gonna do?"

I wasn't sure what to say.

Lil' Larry jumped when Lashaune started calling my name louder. I was okay until I heard Momzie holler just a few seconds later. "Robert? Who is in the house and what is goin' on? ... Robert, everything okay?"

Lil' Larry turned to face me. He looked like someone had hit him over the head with a baseball bat and he couldn't tell which way was up anymore. He took a deep breath, squared his shoulders, opened his mouth as if to speak again, and ran for the back door with the sheet flapping behind him. If I hadn't been about to throw up from nerves, I might have laughed.

My knees shook so bad, I had to grab the wall to keep from falling on my way back up the stairs. "Everything's fine, Momzie," I called about halfway up in hopes of preventing her or Grandpa Ray from coming out of their room to check for themselves.

I went back in the room and grabbed my underwear and jeans off the floor.

"What's up?" I asked Lashaune once I had my pants on.

Lashaune dropped her hands and looked up at me, tears running down her cheeks. "What was that about?" A sob broke her voice.

"Look man, why you trippin'? You know, it's between us. Nobody needs to know."

"Why did you do that with Lil' Larry? Why?"

"C'mon now, what are you talking about? Nothing happened." I wanted her to understand we wouldn't spread it around the neighborhood. We'd be happy to pretend it never happened if she'd go along with it.

"You know what I'm talking about!"

I leaned over and handed her shirt. "Naw, man, I've been here with you the whole time. Ain't nothing unusual happened here."

"No, no, you were sweating and he was bone dry, and I—"

"Aw, you talking crazy now, girl. You must be hungry or tired. Let's get you home so you can get something to eat."

I was willing to say anything I could to calm her down. She might call rape. I was terrified and needed to get her out of the apartment as soon as possible. While most of the guys in the neighborhood would probably laugh if word got out, a woman calling rape would not go over with Momzie or the family—and would certainly cause trouble if the authorities got involved. So I just kept handing her pieces of clothing while she worked on stopping the waterworks.

When I got back home from dropping her off, Lil' Larry was sitting in my room. I was glad to see he was fully clothed. He said he thought she was in missionary when he moved to mount, so he turned her over. A little smile tugged at his lips during his story and his eyes dropped to the floor. I suspected he knew all along she was on her stomach and just wanted her on her back, thinking she'd be cool with it.

I guess I should have bought her an ice cream or something. Made some gesture to ease her worries. But I didn't bother. After a couple days, I figured we were in the clear. Lashaune was a Perry Homes resident. As far as I know, she never said a word.

Chapter 16
Shadows

Grady Memorial Hospital loomed like a pro-football-sized linebacker. At more than nine stories tall, it was the biggest building I'd ever seen—aside from the mall near Misty Waters. Grady, one of the five largest public hospitals in the U.S., was known for being one of the country's busiest level one trauma centers. I stepped gingerly through the doors. The lobby smelled like an army of cleaners had marched through, mopping, spraying, and wiping as they went.

It had happened too many times before. Momzie or Big Larry would let me know Momma Cat had gotten beat up, sick, or in a car accident and was in the hospital. She'd be back home soon enough. Always was. A few times I got to see the aftermath of the beatings up close and personal, wiping away blood and tears from her face. Often nobody at 579 Clarissa knew anything was going on with Cat until someone in the neighborhood let us know she was in the hospital. Momzie would pay her a visit every now and again when she was hospital-bound, but for the most part her recoveries were a solitary undertaking. Someone was always getting shot, beat up, run over, or sick in the 'hood. If we went to the hospital every time, we'd never be home.

Over the last few years, Cat's trips to the hospital were more frequent. At first it was just for a day or two, but shortly after Momma Cat told me about the HIV/AIDS infection, her stays in the hospital grew longer and longer. When Momzie finally came to me and said I better visit, I figured it was serious.

At seventeen, I was a man—a senior in high school. Men take responsibility, I'd told myself when weighing the decision. I didn't know what I was getting into, or what to expect. I just wanted to see my mom, show her my support.

I started pulling on the bottom of my shirt during the ride up in the elevator to the seventh floor. I didn't want to be there. I was frightened. And angry. Being at the hospital meant I was breaking a promise to myself; I wouldn't see Momma Cat anymore. Not after what she'd done the last time I'd seen her several months prior.

* * * * * * * * *

Without a word of warning, Momma Cat grabbed the steering wheel. She gave it a hard turn to the right before I was able to grasp her wrist and stop her. We grappled, scrambling for control of the wheel. The car veered toward the curb.

"What you doin', Cat?" I shouted and wrestled the car back under control.

"I ain't dying alone," she yelled and made another attempt to grab the wheel. "If I'm gonna die, I'm gonna die how I want, not in some hospital bed somewhere."

She's trying to kill me. Throwing an elbow, I hoped it would force her to defend herself and back away from the wheel. It worked.

She stared at me, hatred seeping out her eyes, chest heaving, and hands twitching. It was only a matter of seconds before she tried again.

"Have you went crazy woman? You sit over there and don' move an inch the rest of the way or I swear to God, I will pull this car over and leave you on the curb. I don't care who you are!"

For a few seconds, I thought she'd lunge. I kept one eye on her and one on the road, slowing the car to ten miles an hour just in case. Suddenly, she deflated. Exhaling like a flotation device with an open plug, she crumpled. Momma Cat folded her hands in her lap and dropped her head to her chest. She didn't say a single word the rest of the way to 579 Clarissa.

I marched ahead of her into the house, briefly told Big Larry what she'd done, and went upstairs to watch television. A small part of me realized, through her drug and disease-riddled body, her heart was issuing a cry for help. I was too angry to give it much thought—or an ounce of sympathy. I don't know who took Cat back to the rooming house that night. I didn't care.

* * * * * * * * *

Momma Cat didn't say much when I walked in to the hospital room. Her face was covered with a surgical mask. The nurse had warned me about it when I stopped at the nurses' station on the way in to double-check the room number. She told me the mask was to protect her against germs. Part of the cruel irony of AIDS, was at the time when an individual needs their loved ones the most, too much close contact could be a real physical danger.

"How you doin', Cat? You okay?" I asked from the doorway.

I walked over and pulled up a chair to sit next to the bed. Momma Cat watched me silently. She nodded and blinked a couple times. I figured it meant she was doing okay. For a while, I sat there talking about school and what different family members were up to. Tiffany was crawling so fast none of us could keep up. I told her how I was writing skits for the senior play and planning to perform some as well, and I was still tearing it up on the football field every Friday night. I told her about my trip downtown in the wake of the Rodney King verdict to express my frustrations alongside thousands of others; promised her I didn't take part in any of the destruction accompanying the demonstrations. Although it had been months since the verdict, I felt the need to tell her and hoped she would appreciate my activism.

I didn't tell Momma Cat all the details, just the ones I was proud of. The Archer High principal came over the loudspeakers and asked students to avoid the demonstrations following the decision to acquit four Los Angeles Police Department officers of assaulting Rodney King. Across Atlanta, members of the black community were raging against the unfairness of the verdict, complaining it was the latest in a long string of injustices against black people by the system. Perry Homes residents felt the same. The Rodney King verdict united people who were normally divided by drugs, money, and the drive for individual survival.

I hopped on a bus after school. Downtown, the mood was dark. Demonstrators decided to march toward Buckhead, a wealthier neighborhood. The police rode in on horses to prevent protesters from leaving downtown. As I ran through the streets toward the Omni train station to hop a train home, I saw cops throwing people into paddy wagons and prayed I wouldn't end up in jail. I shook the entire ride home, convinced the police would stop the train and pull me off. The adventure had been an attempt to express my feelings on politics, but it was an empty expression of how upset I was with the system. I achieved nothing.

After a few minutes I exhausted everything I could think of to say to Cat. I just sat there quietly holding her hand, marveling at the fact that this was the quietest, calmest time we'd spent alone together in years. She wasn't yelling or cursing, pinching or slapping. There was no Blacky with us. No demon. No evidence of any evil spirits. Just Momma Cat lying in a bed, looking skinny and worn years before her time.

"I love you, Cat," I blurted out.

She tightened her grip on my hand and mumbled through the mask that she loved me too.

It may have been the first time I ever said the words, "I love you," out loud to my mother. I loved Momma Cat with all my heart, through good and bad. I didn't know whether I would ever find the strength to forgive Cat all her trespasses, and if I could, how long it might take to reach that point. But there was still a lot of love for her in my aching heart. I didn't know how many more chances, if any, I'd have to tell her. And she needed to know.

It was the last time I ever saw my mother.

My childhood home at apartment 579 of building 2163 Clarissa Drive, a three bedroom apartment in Perry Homes; one of the largest housing projects in the Southeast. Top left is the window to my, momma Cat's and Tracy's bedroom. Top right is the window to the bathroom; My place of refuge and meditation.

Neighborhood kids standing outside of my childhood home in front of my '86 Ford Tempo.

Me at age 4, 2nd from left, sitting with cousins and brother Tracy far right on the sofa in my grandmother's living room at 579.

The ceiling of our bedroom at 579. This picture taken around my senior year of high school

Me at age 6.

Me in Ms. Warren's 4th grade class at
C.M. Pitts Elementary School.

My older brother Tracy
at around age 11 or 12.

Me at age 13 in Washington DC
on a 7th grade school field trip.

Me at approximately age 16 standing in doorway of 2163 after football practice. My mom Catherine ("Cat") is sitting in chair and my aunt Brenda is sitting on the step in front of her.

My grandmother Ethelrine ("Momzie") standing out-front of our apartment.

My uncle Larry outfront of our home at 2163.

Family picture at my uncle Lamar's home. Top row from left - My uncles Larry, Raymond, Johnny Ray and Lamar "Pop". Bottom row from left - My aunt Patricia "Pat", grandmother Ethelrine, my aunt Brenda and my mom "Cat".

Me at about age 10 or 11 with my paternal aunt Tina and cousin John "John-John." Just leaving church service I'm sporting my cousin's Sunday's best.

Me at age 18 with my brother Tracy standing in the entrance to the kitchen at my grandma's apartment at 2163.

Me at age 9 in my grandma's livingroom admiring family trophies. We had a family full of athletes.

My grandfather Ray standing beside his car out-front of 2163.

My mother Catherine "Cat" out-front of our home at 2163 months before her death.

Me at age 20 with my brother Tracy in the living room of 2163.

The backyard of 2163 and pathway where I pooped my pants. There were many violent crimes and deaths that took place along the path.

View from front door of 2163. Directly behind trees on right was the location for the city dump where the most obscene odors navigated to our front porch.

Me at age 18 in the backyard of 2163, shortly after my mom's death.

Running the track of Archer High School in preparation for my football season at Kentucky State University. One of the few things that helped me escape the insanity of the hoodlife and cope with the loss of my mother "Cat".

The kitchen pantry and laundry area at 2163.

Me recuperating from a football injury. This picture was taken days within the near crack addict attack incident at Church's Chicken.

Our football practice field at Samuel Howard Archer High (SHA).

The back of our High School. (SHA) Picture taken from the practice football field.

Me at age 18 at a Christmas party "The Player's Ball" hosted by my grandparents Ray and Ethelrine Many parties preceded but this was the 1st celebration without my mom "Cat."

High School graduation weeks after my mother's death.

Me and Commaleta visiting my grandparents and childhood home in Perry Homes while on Spring break of our sophomore year of college.

Commaleta at age 15.

Picture of a Subway, my 1st place of employment.

The front counter of the Buckhead Subway where I worked.

93

Me at University of Georgia (UGA) helping to build the set for our production "Fences."

Me receiving congrats from my close friend and roommate Erroyl McGinty and then fiancé Commaleta at the Morton Theater after the performance of "Fences;" a UGA - BTE production.

Me at UGA's Multi-Cultural Arts Center Rehearsal Hall.

Apartment in Athens on Church Street that I shared with my roommate and close friend Erroyl. My then fiancé Commaleta later joined us during her last month of pregnancy with our first child Heavven. Picture was taken from the parking lot of building.

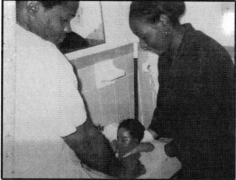

Me and Commaleta learning to bathe our 1st born, Heavven Désja in the bathroom sink of our apartment.

Me in Florida the week of the Outback Bowl. This picture was taken the day after the Taco Bell incident between me and Commaleta.

This was taken shortly after the announcer called my name to enter onto the field at Sanford Stadium during the UGA homecoming game of 1996.

Pictures of me as different characters in Georgia Public Television's "Transitions" - 1998.

The grand opening of our costume shop. Characters were me as Shrek, my wife as Batgirl, colleagues as Batman and Spiderman, my sister-n-law as Ninja, my brother-n-law as Cat In The Hat our daughters as lil Spidy and Snow White.

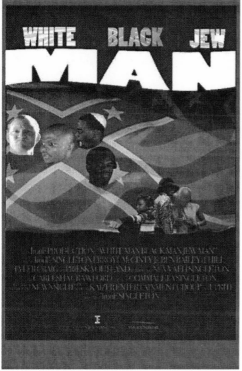

The poster for my independent film "White Man Black Man Jew Man" (WBJ). This film was shot with no budget at our home in Georgia with minimal equipment and amazing and dedicated talent. From left to right, Ben Bailey, me, Erroyl McGinty, Demarcus Hill, Nevvaeh Singleton, Tyler Craig, Prieska Outland.

The backdrop and poster for my one man stage production - "IronE The Resurrected."

Me in a dramatic scene as IronE.

Me playing my alter ego referred to as Alter "E."

Me playing the character of my mother "Cat."

My wife, stage manager, sound tech and personal manager sharing her critique after the close of our first show at the 14th Street Playhouse. I only had about 5 attendees in the audience that night. "The show must go on."

Me during my days as a track coach.

Me as a sports official.

Me as "Homer" for the Atlanta Braves.

Me performing as "Okie Dokie" the clown at a kid 's birthday party.

99

Our son and youngest, Ethereal Zephyr ("EZ") at 4 months. Everyone says he looked exactly like I did when I was a baby.

Me holding our middle child Nevvaeh Celeste only days old.

Me with our eldest child Heavven Désja at 2 years

Me and my wife Commaleta in New York at the Premiere of The Blind Side.

The Singleton Family Winter 2010.

The Singleton Family Winter 2012.

The community previously known as Misty Waters (now Spring Valley) where my paternal grandmother, aunt and cousin lived and I visited frequently as a child between the ages of 8 and 12 years of age.

Image of me ...sharing my childhood memories of Misty Waters with my co-author Juliette Terzieff during a recent visit to the Spring Valley community.

The building on McDaniel Street in Atlanta where my mom "Cat" resided during her final years. Sitting in the Cadillac Cimarron on this street is where she told me she had HIV. She also died in this building.

Chapter 17
Light

Momzie got the call on a Saturday. It was May 8, 1993. The kind of late springtime evening where you throw open the windows and sip a glass of cool, sweet tea as the breeze comes in. None of us were ready for the shadow that fell over 579 Clarissa.

Momzie relayed the news, speaking in a low monotone. Momma Cat's current male friend, Randy, had come home from work to find her laying on the kitchen floor in a daze. When he asked Cat how long she'd been there, her reply was little more than a moan. He picked Momma Cat up, took her the short distance to the bedroom, and covered her with a blanket, promising to bring back something to eat.

"She wa' just a skin and bones," Randy told Momzie.

Cat hadn't been taking her medicine for several months while she continued to party. Searching around the kitchen for a clean plate to put the small portion of leftover meat and vegetables he'd found, Randy heard Momma Cat let out a series of short raspy coughs. She stopped hacking and he headed in to check on her. Momma Cat was dead.

"I ain't got nothin' left in me for it," Momzie told Big Larry as he gulped in breaths of air. "I done all my crying so many times for so damned long, at least, well, at least she at peace now."

Larry stood in front of Momzie, tears pooling in the corner of his eyes. Despite his size, he seemed so small—shrunk down by his grief to the size of a young boy. Larry was overwhelmed by the gravity of the situation and looked to his momma for comfort. Momzie turned and faced the window. I stepped tentatively past the couch on my way up to my room, glancing briefly at Grandpa Ray. He had his face raised toward the ceiling and murmured what sounded like prayers. Big Larry squared his shoulders and took deep calming breaths, which sounded more like sighs.

Momzie, Grandpa Ray and Big Larry already accepted what I could not fathom, even though I saw the truth etched on their faces. Momma Cat had lost too many pieces of herself along the way—fighting a years-long battle with demons determined to destroy her. She'd fought so hard, for so long, somehow we all thought she'd just keep fighting. *How did it come to this?*

* * * * * * * * *

The adults scattered and reappeared as individuals over the next couple of hours after placing phone calls to relatives and friends, making burial arrangements. I mostly hung out upstairs alone in our bedroom. My bedroom. The space I'd shared for so many years with Cat and Tracy. They were both gone now. It was a tough fight to find some balance amid the perfect storm of emotions battering my mind. I only had the one clear thought since sitting down.

Staring at nothing in the dark room, I occasionally glanced out the window to the night sky. I had neglected to turn on the light. I felt … numb. I wasn't really in my body. I stared at him from across the room—a silent peeping Tom, watching the other Robert struggle to focus on one feeling or thought, not caring whether he succeeded. I didn't want to feel and blanketed myself in the numbness.

Momma Cat would be buried at Lincoln Cemetery, where my great grandparents and other deceased relatives took their final rest. I couldn't remember which of the adults in the apartment made the announcement.

I forced myself to take a deep breath and rose to pad over to the bathroom. There had been so many times I stood there staring into the mirror, venting, dreaming, assuring myself everything would be okay—I was gonna be somebody. Even if I stood there for hours, I couldn't come up with one thing to say to get my head on straight this time. I wiped my eyes with a wad of toilet paper and headed back to my room.

Conversation ebbed and flowed downstairs, depending on who was in the living room. I caught bits and pieces of it as I continued to stare into the darkness outside my bedroom window. There was a lot of talk among the women about how pretty Momma Cat was. How if one caught her unawares, they were blessed with the rare opportunity to see and hear an angel. Especially when she was braiding her hair. She would almost always hum or sing while she twirled strands of hair. If you were fool enough to compliment Cat, she'd blush like a schoolgirl and push you away with a smile. In a particularly good mood, Cat could be found dancing to the radio a little while she worked in the kitchen.

The only thing I heard from Aunt Brenda over the sound of my cousins, Momzie, and friends conversing, was her crying. All of the reminiscing just seemed to make her cry even harder. I felt Aunt Brenda's pain. My throat tightened so severely, I had to really work to take a breath.

The Cat they spoke of was one I had seen less and less of as the years passed. I couldn't even remember the last time I'd seen her smile.

There was also plenty of talk about the headaches Momma Cat gave the family. She'd knock on the door in the middle of the night, screaming and waking up the entire household at midnight, one, or two in the morning. It'd happened too many times to count during her last year. It almost became a routine. When we all got out of bed, I would beg Momzie from the top of the stairs not to open the door. Momzie, in turn, would threaten to call the cops if Momma Cat didn't take her hollering somewhere else.

I ventured out of my room and was halfway down the stairs when Momzie began telling a story that stopped me in my tracks.

Despite her promise not to let Momma Cat in the house, Momzie had opened the door on one of Cat's recent midnight visits. It was the middle of winter, just after New Year's.

"After she was done carrying on, she quieted down and said 'Miss Rine I'm so cold, won't you open up? Momma?'" Momzie recalled, her voice quavering a little. When she opened the door, she found her daughter shivering on the stoop in a thin spring jacket. There was no Blacky in sight, just her daughter, just Cat. Momzie's desire to let her in was held at bay by the fear she had of her offspring. She prayed some of the heat from inside would travel out the open door and warm Momma Cat. She embraced her daughter. After a few minutes, she turned her away.

"How terrible a thing is it when you can't even let your own daughter into the house?" Momzie's shrill voice made me cringe. Nobody answered.

Somewhere in the midst of the story, Tracy showed up. Seeing him in the doorway wide-eyed and ravenous with anger, he reminded me so much of Momma Cat. What I wouldn't have given for her to be standing there, to launch a tickle attack on me. I'd be happy and laugh, even though her cold hands always made me shiver. *God*, I thought, watching Big Larry's attempts to calm Tracy, *right now, I'd even take some of her pinching and slapping.* I'd be a good boy and keep quiet even if she hurt me, so Momzie wouldn't hear and yell at her to leave. If I could just get her back, I'd find a way to make things right.

"I want you boys to come with me," Aunt Brenda said in a steadier tone than I'd heard her use since she entered 579 Clarissa.

Nobody said a word when Aunt Brenda got up to lead Tracy past me to the stairs and started climbing. Tracy and I barely looked at each other. She walked straight in to the bedroom Momma Cat, Tracy, and I had once shared and ordered us to close the door without even turning around. The moment I crossed the threshold into my room, my gut began to rise. I put out a hand to steady myself on the dresser and pursed my lips tight. Everything from my little intestines up threatened to make a projectile exit from my mouth. Tracy shut the door.

"You two need to listen to me, now." Aunt Brenda sat on the bed where Momma Cat used to sleep. Her color was blotchy and she'd started crying again. She opened her arms to beckon us forward. Neither of us had moved away from the door. "C'mon, now, come sit wit' me." Hanging out on Momma Cat's old bed was one of the last things in the world I wanted to do. Aunt Brenda swayed under the weight of her emotions, struggling to keep a smile on her face despite the circumstances. We had no choice but to answer her summons and sit, one of us on each side of her.

Her voice shook. "Y'all need to stick t'gether now, it's just the two of ya. You're all you got. That's it. Cat's gone. She gone!" Without warning Aunt Brenda put her arms around us and dragged us against her shoulders in a giant hug. I heard her whispering a little prayer over the pounding of my heart. I joined her silently with one of my own.

We stayed there, locked in a three-way hug. Aunt Brenda talked through her tears about family, love, and forgiveness. She talked about becoming men and taking responsibility. Momma Cat would be watching down on us with love and pride, Brenda assured, and her spirit would always be with us. We said a prayer for Momma Cat, that she find a peaceful rest.

Neither Tracy nor I moved when Aunt Brenda got up and left the room. He didn't seem to know what to say any more than I did. I wanted to tell him what I felt, but I couldn't find the words to describe the agony. I wanted him to tell me everything would be all right. Those were words he'd never speak. I stole a look at my older brother. He looked diminished—sitting there hunched over, eyes bloodshot and swollen from crying. Yet somehow I felt closer to him than I had in years. He alone understood the anguish I was feeling without me saying a single word, and I loved him for it.

Tracy stood up fast; like a puppeteer yanked invisible strings attached to his shoulders. He put his hand on my arm and gave it a squeeze before walking out the door.

If I had known my worst fears about where his chosen path was leading him would come true, I would have reached out to grab hold of him and never let go. In a few months, Tracy would be doing what he was dealing—snorting cocaine and doing other drugs like a pro. Not long after, it would land him in prison—a place he would end up repeatedly over the years. He got a full grill on his front teeth, tattoos too many to count, and chains thicker than his fingers. The demon Blacky, which had torn my mother apart, had set its sights firmly on my brother.

* * * * * * * * *

Tracy's departure left me alone with my thoughts. They were dark—devoid of light or hope. Darker thoughts than I ever remember having before, darker than the night sky outside the window.

"Why?" I yelled. "Why did you take her away, God? When I a'ready ain't got nothin'? What is the use? What is my purpose? I'm supposed to be somebody, right?" The questions erupted from my lips faster than my brain could frame them. My anger rushed out in an unintelligible roar. I felt sick. *Disrespecting God? On the day your mother died?* I was lost, more so than any drug-addled junkie out on the street. My despair deepened.

By the time I regained a tremulous sense of control, my T-shirt was soaked through with tears. I felt dried out, used up … tired. The exhaustion afforded me the opportunity to converse with God in a manner more in tune with the level of respect He deserved. It wasn't right, but it was the best I could do.

I knew God had a plan, at least I thought He did. We were not meant to understand His plan. I had my own plan to focus on. Graduation was only a couple of weeks away. I wanted to work all summer before heading to college to continue my education and play football. Things needed to be made right with Commaleta. I wanted to take care of her. In return she would take care of me. We'd build a life together. Far away from the drugs, violence, and death prowling the streets of Perry Homes like a wolf pack.

"But is that what you want of me? Am I right?" I asked Him.

From the time I was nine, I placed my faith in "the plan." Even if I occasionally stepped off the path, it was always there as a guiding force.

Every year around Martin Luther King Jr.'s birthday they aired "The Boy King" on television, telling the life story of the civil rights leader. Even as a boy, King Jr. had a dream to unite the world through truth and love because it was God's plan, He'd told him so. There was a song in the show about holding on to your dreams and never letting go. Each year I anticipated the show's airing. The song's lyrics rang profoundly true to my heart and my spiritual essence. I knew the plan I envisioned had also come from a higher power. If He could talk to the young King, why couldn't He talk to me? My confusion and sadness were profound.

Everything was lost. In the span of a minute, up turned down, down turned up, and somehow inside was out. I lifted my head toward the sky and made my plea. "Either I'm gonna kill somebody or they gonna kill me because I give up. What am I doin' heh? Why, why am I here? Please, God, please *help* me. Show me the light."

And right at that moment, He did. Like a fast-motion pale sunrise, white light spread across the wall and part of the ceiling. The corner position of our home, and where our bedroom was, made light shows a frequent occurrence as cars came down the street. Having it happen in that precise moment? To a poor, black, uneducated nobody like me, with battered dreams of being somebody, it seemed like the answer I was looking for. My pain was far from over. The loss of Momma Cat, I understood instinctively, would stay with me and impact the rest of my life.

But I knew what I had to do—keep following "the plan."

Chapter 18
Hustle Man

I loved everything about the University of Georgia campus and the city it resided in—Athens, Georgia. Anywhere you looked, the sprawling campus teemed with the promise of a bright future. There were few street brawls here, and no guns. There were drugs and alcohol, but they were recreational vehicles for the most part, not a way of life.

I rode the campus North-South bus between classes, practice, and my room in Myers Hall. Sometimes I'd stay on the bus past the stop where I should get off, riding around the campus and looking out the windows with a smile on my face. The route took passengers across the sprawling campus. It passed landmarks including the University Village housing with Myers, Mary Lyndon, and Rutherford Halls; the Tate Student Center; the College of Veterinary Medicine; and the Lamar Dodd School of Art. Campus buildings—which ranged from red brick housing to ornately decorated structures reflecting the areas of studies within—were spaced out with large lawns and towering trees between them. At all times of the day, students scurried to and from classes, backpacks stuffed with books. Many of them sported a portable CD player pumping music into their ears. There were black kids, whites, Asians, Latinos. Straight kids, gay kids, jocks, science geeks, and goths. Everyone found a way to fit into the multifaceted fabric of UGA life.

Even though I was well into the second year of my studies, the environment of the university campus continued to astound me. Folks in Perry Homes scrambled to have enough to survive and looked despondently toward a grim future they could see all too clearly. In contrast, everyone at the university was working, studying, and sprinting toward a future of their own making. They had choices and opportunities. I couldn't count how many times I sat outside the Tate Student Center, soaking up the sun and hum of activity around me, and thought about Perry Homes, Momma Cat, and Tracy—who was incarcerated. The old neighborhood was not a part of my life anymore and would never be again, I promised myself. I was out, free. And I wished with all my heart that Momma Cat, Tracy, and the rest of my family, could've been there with me.

I was a proud member of the UGA Bulldogs football team—a division one college team—and working hard to earn degrees in Theatre and in Speech Communications. At UGA I had the opportunity to be a pro-class football player. Every moment I could spare was spent training and honing my skills. I had focus, determination to achieve goals I'd always hoped for, but wondered if I'd ever get the chance.

Commaleta and I were together again. I'd foolishly asked her to marry me shortly after I turned eighteen. She refused because she knew—better than I did—that I was not ready. So I kept asking. She had gone off to West Georgia College; I started my university career at Kentucky State University. It was a truly lovely institution, where I played ball and continued to explore the enjoyment of acting I'd discovered in my senior year of high school. I participated in KSU's production of *Sophisticated Ladies*. But I missed Georgia, my family and Commaleta. On top of everything else, I knew if I wanted to make it to the National Football League, UGA was a better place for me than KSU, so I sought a transfer to UGA. Soon after, Commaleta did the same.

When I began my university career as a freshman at KSU, I wanted to prove to myself I had tenacity, the ability to grow and develop. My plan was to give up something I liked every year for the span of one year, kind of a New Year's resolution to reinforce my personal sense of discipline. I narrowed my choices down to giving up beef or pork.

The year before, I watched *Macolm X* and had gone to see Dr. Khalid Muhammad, the assistant minister to Louis Farrakhan, speak on campus. Spike Lee's character in the movie, a guy called Shorty, had said he didn't think he could be Muslim if white women and pork were not allowed. Now, I wasn't about to go that far. I didn't want to seem disrespectful to women by making sexually related comments. However, when Muhammad talked about the pig—how disgusting an animal it was—I stood and asked for an explanation.

"Brother, you are lost. You need a better understanding of the word," he shouted over the crowd and began to preach. "It's okay brother, you going to be alright. You just ignorant."

I didn't pay much heed right away, embarrassed by his fifteen-minute response to my question. But what he said stuck with me, and when I made my decision, pork lost out. I wanted to see if I had enough discipline to make my goal—to be pork-free for a year. For someone who loved pork chops and chittlins as much as I did, it was no small challenge.

The next year when I transferred to the University of Georgia, I kept the pork abstinence going. That year I added beer and alcohol to the out-of-bounds list. The year after, it was sweets. It made me stronger. I knew if I could do this, if I could get through a whole year not consuming something I enjoyed by choice, then I could do anything. By the time I hit the end of my college career, I still wasn't back to eating pork. Most of the pork dishes I'd grown up loving were prepared with a lot of fat and were extremely unhealthy eating choices. A quick look at the rate of high blood pressure, obesity, diabetes, and heart disease among African Americans was enough to convince me to reexamine my diet on a more permanent basis. Pork lost out, my health won, and I haven't eaten it since.

It was a time for making changes, for plotting the course of the life I wanted to live, the goals I wanted to achieve. I didn't waste a single minute. In addition to coursework and football, I threw myself into the UGA theater program to round out my campus activities. I'd reached out to Greg, my old boss at Subway, to let him know I was still available to work during breaks and holidays. I was working part-time at a restaurant in the Athens area at the same time. I also made a few extra bucks on the side selling cologne, incense, underwear, and any other legal product I could get my hands on. For my efforts on and off the field, my Dawg teammates renamed me "The Hustle Man." It was a nickname and a way of life that followed me well past my university years.

My success within this amazing new world didn't ensure I wouldn't encounter darker elements. It was just a different shade of evil than I was used to.

Shortly after I transferred, I received a phone call so out of place in UGA's melting pot environment, it was several minutes after the call ended before I could react properly.

It was Saturday evening, and I was finishing up a bit of coursework before meeting up with some friends. The voice on the other end of the phone responded to my hello with a series of racial epithets so vulgar, so ferocious, even a street thug's insides would flinch. He rattled them off like an auctioneer taking bids, giving me little opportunity to say more than, "What the …?" when he stopped to take a quick breath. In the span of sixty seconds he called me every slur in the books, and a few new ones. He topped it off by threatening to piss on the grave of my mother.

Afterward, I wondered if it was some of the guys playing a joke. In my gut, I knew better. The hostility rebuilt parts of my Perry Homes mindset I thought were forever consigned to an emotional landfill in the far recesses of my mind.

I was angry and a little bit bitter about it. Did Charlayne Hunter Gault—the first African American woman to attend UGA—encounter many racially-charged incidents during her time in the 1960s? She must have dealt with a lot of them. I prayed on it, reminded myself to be thankful for the blessings I had and keep working.

For the first few months we shared a living space, my roommate and I seemed to get along okay. We didn't talk much beyond basic daily pleasantries, but it was in no way awkward. Both of us had a full load of classes and then some. He was in a special honor's program, and I played football and worked on theater projects. But not too long after the phone call incident, we got into a scrap that brought home all the stories Big Larry told me about discrimination and racial hatred he experienced growing up. There was at least one good thing about living in Perry Homes, almost the entire population was the same ethnicity. Racism was something I had only peripheral experience with until I hit the real world outside the streets full time.

I woke the moment the overhead light switched on, and rolled over to look at my clock. It was after one in the morning. My roommate sat at his desk, ruffling papers and opening a book. I asked him politely if he would turn the light off and work using his desk lamp. I needed to be up early the next morning.

"You had on the light when I was trying to sleep," he responded.

It took me a few seconds to figure out what he was talking about. Earlier in the evening my roommate had come back to our shared space to take a nap while I was studying. It had been about eight o'clock, a time I considered reasonable to have the light on. Besides, I didn't own a desk lamp like he did.

"But you neva said nuthin' 'bout it. I coulda gone to the student center or library or sumpin' if you'd tol' me it was a botha," I said. For some inexplicable reason my speech reverted to straight up 'hood talk.

"No. Well, it's on now and I have to study."

"Well, I cain't sleep like that."

My roommate shrugged and flipped a page in his book. He hadn't turned around once to face me during this exchange. It bothered me.

"I'm gonna ask you again to turn off that light, man."

When he didn't respond, I got out of bed and stomped over to turn off the light myself. No sooner had I laid back down and pulled the covers up, he turned the light on. Without a word, I stood and walked over to the light switch. I flipped it off and stood there for a few seconds before heading back to bed. My roommate got up from his chair and turned it on again. I waited until he returned to his desk and started studying to get out of bed.

We flipped the light on and off a few more times before my anger reached a boiling point.

"Look, man, I ain't gonna do this all night." I marched over to his desk and snatched his books away. "Don't you turn that light on again," I warned him and I hopped into my bed.

"You ape. Stupid monkey," he hollered.

I jumped out of bed in a fury and lunged at him, trying to provoke him into hitting me so I could knock him out and get some peace. He threw up his arms to protect his face and ducked, simultaneously throwing a knee kick and hitting himself in the face. We both stopped in shock. His nose began to drip blood on to his shirt.

"You see what your violence caused? It's always bloodshed with you people!" He headed for the door.

I stood there shaking. *I'm gone. As soon as they see that blood on that white boy, I'm gone.* His books dropped from my hands and tumbled to the floor. I backed up and sat heavily down on the bed to wait.

He came back in a couple minutes with the RA—residents' assistant—who listened to both sides of the story and decided we were both to blame for the incident. As angry as I was, I respected my roommate for admitting the bloodletting was a result of his own action and not trying to play it off like I hit him. But I was also sad. I could no longer live with a man who thought of me as "one of those people." He seemed fairly cool, never acted weird or anything, yet there had been racism lurking beneath the surface the entire time.

We ended up at a judicial hearing and were both put on probation. For me, the school's disciplinary action was a secondary punishment. The real pain I felt from the incident lay in coming to terms with the continuing undercurrent of racism in society. I'd often felt out of place in Perry Homes, dreaming of something different and knowing if I believed in myself and God's plan, I would find a way to succeed and escape the fate awaiting so many of the people I knew. This was different. Intellectually I knew any racial vitriol I might encounter was the result of ignorance or fear, and in my heart I knew the only way to counter it was through love. I was just learning to find my place in this big new world outside the 'hood. The behavior of my roommate made me feel like an outsider in a kaleidoscope of humanity that had previously felt so welcoming.

Chapter 19
Red and Black

They knew it was coming. As the bell tolled, a roar of approval rose from around the stadium as the crowd awaited the voice that would blanket them in UGA pride. When the tumult began to wane, the announcer let them have it.

"Ladies and gentlemen! If your blood runs red and black, get on your feet and let's make some Sanford stadium noooooooiiise!"

I waited my turn in the tunnel. The crowd cheered at the announcement of each Georgia Bulldog player. We were all decked out in red and white jerseys, mine with the number twenty-three on the back. It was the fall of 1996. As a team, we were ready to tear apart any squad that dared opposed us. I was on my way toward being a professional football player. I was also on my way to being a father. There was a world of work ahead of me.

* * * * * * * * * *

Every day, every hour I spent working out, running scrimmages, or suiting up for a game was pure joy. Football had always been that way for me. Back in high school, I was only able to enjoy fleeting moments during Friday night games and practice sessions. My happiness in those days had been tempered by the knowledge, when the final whistle blew I'd have to go back to Perry Homes. At UGA the dark chapter of my life was over, things were changing. When I finished my work on the practice field or in the weight room, there was coursework to be done, lines for theater productions to learn, and life lessons to experience.

Just before the school year started, Commaleta discovered she was pregnant. The knowledge we would soon be parents meant I needed to work even harder than I had been to ensure we were in a position to provide a better upbringing for our child than I had experienced. The responsibility didn't scare me, it propelled me.

We started to search for off-campus housing and I picked up extra shifts at work. Commaleta wasn't quite convinced as I was that I was ready for family life.

I had already made a failed attempt at cementing an engagement to marry, but felt it was time to try again. I proposed to her over the spring break of our sophomore year while visiting her at West Georgia College. The on again, off again waltz that had characterized our relationship throughout high school had concluded almost concurrently with my spiritual epiphany after Cat's death and transition to college. I knew the distance between us when I was at KSU helped make my sexual indulgences easier to keep under her radar, but it also made it imperative I commit solidly to Commaleta. Her options for finding a suitable replacement companion would broaden the moment we went off to college and I wasn't foolish enough to risk losing the woman that I knew God intended for me by failing to secure our relationship before our onward and upward journey.

I didn't know what I was doing, or how I would do it, or if I would be rejected as she had done when I popped the question to her during our phone conversations in the past. I was clearly more focused and more mature at this stage in my life, especially compared to the fast-track player lifestyle that I had been accustomed to during my upbringing. I pulled up memories of the glamorized proposals I had viewed in movie and television love scenes. While Commaleta was not the type that cared much about extravagant presentations or gifts, I decided I should make an effort to make it special.

In the sunset light of her dorm room, with sweaty quivering palms and shaky legs, I got down on one knee and presented her a teddy bear with a ring attached to a small pillow. When she accepted through tears, my heart regained its normal rhythm and the return of a steady flow of oxygen saved me from what was sure to be a flat out panic attack. Though I was still in denial about the deceptions looming over our relationship due to my ongoing infidelities, it felt right. But our emotions were in a knot woven so tightly, we ended up in an argument that later convinced Commaleta, the timing was still premature.

Now over a year later with a restored engagement to marry, Commaleta choked back words of doubts that remained and shared the news of our expectancy.

Like the rest of the student body, my football teammates came from all over the place—a variety of upbringings and traditions. There was Richard Seymour, who went on to win three Super Bowl rings with the New England Patriots before a knee injury ended his pro ball career. Wide receiver Hines Ward won a couple Super Bowls with the Pittsburgh Steelers and was named to the Pro-Bowl numerous times. Roland "Champ" Bailey went on to amass more Pro Bowl appearances—eleven—than any other cornerback in NFL history.

Whether it was my football teammates or other aspiring actors, we were all reaching toward similar goals. We were living our passions, reaching for our dreams. Everyone focused on learning more about their chosen field, and how to best prepare for success. It was an approach I'd only experienced on the football field before then. From the time I was a small child, I was determined to break out of the 'hood life laid out before me and many of my peers as the only option for the future. Although my personal roadmap was geared toward a career in the NFL, at university I realized the goals and strategic approach of football could be applied to other aspects of life.

The majority of my football-related hours were spent around Butts-Mehre Heritage Hall—a building housing the sports medicine team, a workout area with more weights and machines than I'd ever known existed, locker and shower areas, meeting rooms, and memorabilia of Dawgs who had come before. Outside was a practice field, decked out with the large black and white "G" representing the school on either end.

Some days after practice I would stand midfield and marvel that I was standing where greats like Fran Tarkenton and Herschel Walker had taken instrumental steps toward the same dream I was chasing. It was heaven to me, and such an honor. The realization that I was playing for the UGA Bulldogs brought me to tears more than once. They were different tears than I had shed in high school during my nighttime visits to the Archer High field. My frustrations had been replaced by pride, a sense of achievement, and hope for the future. I had come so far. Crossed entire worlds in my quest to make a reality out of the vision in my head. Yet, at the same time, it was only the beginning of what I hoped to achieve.

For most of my football career I'd focused on playing defense, but switched during my time at UGA to running back. Whenever I'd go home to visit the family at 579 Clarissa, people would compliment me for playing with the Bulldogs, be in awe at my achievement. I felt their pride, but I knew the coming years would show them all how much more I could do.

I was still consigned to the scout team, which meant I wasn't a starting player. Scout teams were responsible for emulating opposing teams for starting players. Coaches used them to develop younger players, prepare them to eventually replace starters who graduated. The coach had spoken to me on several occasions, remarking how he loved my hustle and work ethic, and urged me to keep at it. There was a part of me that was frustrated to still be on the scout team in my junior year, but I had no thought for changing course. I was the Hustle Man. My dreams would take me further than UGA if I worked hard and kept my faith in God.

* * * * * * * * *

The noise of the capacity crowd shook the ground I stood on while I waited for the announcer to call my name. I bounced back and forth from one foot to the other, shaking my hips and shoulders in a little dance timed to the rhythmic snapping of my fingers. The announcer called out Hines Ward and Dax Langley. I watched my teammates welcome them onto the field when they sprinted out the tunnel.

I began to jog when I heard the announcer say, "From Atlanta, number 23 …."

I emerged into the bright lights of Sanford Stadium. The crowd reacted.

"… Robert Singleton!"

I ran down the line, slapping hands with my fellow Dawgs and saw my path clearly laid out before me.

Chapter 20
Identity Swap

Lying in bed with our firstborn, Heavven, cradled asleep on my chest felt exactly as her name implied. We were home. Parents. Caretakers for this little baby girl. Guardians not only for our own futures, but hers as well. I bought a car—fifteen hundred dollars for a silver Ford Tempo. I made the decision to cheat less on Commaleta and seek out people who were in long-term relationships to understand how they were managing their lives. The exhaustion from weeks and weeks of sleep deprivation at the hands of our infant daughter became a mark of progress for me. With each passing day, she was growing—and so were we.

For the first time in our lives, Commaleta and I had a place we together were responsible for. It was a two-bedroom apartment on Church Street, nestled on the ground floor of a brown and white brick-faced building not far from the UGA campus. We shared the apartment with my friend Erroyl, whose endless generosity and friendship continue to inspire me today.

The space included a nice little sitting area adjacent to the kitchen. Sufficient for our secondhand couch, a recliner, and television-VCR set up—just the right amount of space for a family of three and a couple friends to hang out. We spent hours there— Heavven watching Sesame Street and Usher videos while we read school assignments. Our bedroom served as sleeping quarters, nursery, and a study lounge all rolled into one. We placed the baby's crib between our twin-sized bed and the closet. A card from the hospital with our daughter's full name, Heavven Desja Dailah-nai Singleton, was taped to the front of the crib's headboard. A picture of Minnie Mouse hung on the wall above.

We had enough space between the foot of the bed and the computer desk to put a small chair. We placed milk crates on either side of the desk for books, our printer, and other school supplies to complete the study area.

The only problem with our Church Street abode was the rats. Anytime it got quiet inside the apartment, we heard them sneaking from behind the walls to search for food in the kitchen. They had the good sense to scamper out of sight if one of us stepped into the kitchen area and switched on the light. But on the nights Commaleta arrived home after sunset, she'd come running in the door screaming about swarms of rats at the dumpsters near our parking spaces.

Theater productions at school with both the Black Theatrical Ensemble and the standard UGA theatre program were opening my eyes to the struggle of others. It gave me a greater understanding of African Americans and their battles within American society and helped me develop a mature way of thinking about behavior and respect. BTE productions—based almost exclusively on works by black artists—were such a contrast to productions like *Angels in America, West Side Story* and *Dangerous Liaisons* which were done by the theatre department. By doing both, I was not only expanding my own knowledge, but giving the audiences a chance to add to their education rosters.

Fences by August Wilson was the first production I did with the BTE after arriving at UGA. It was the story of a black family in the 1950s and the struggles the father experienced trying to repair relationships with his wife and son while keeping the family afloat financially through hard times. I played the son, Cory Maxson, who had a limited relationship with his father, Troy, because the elder Maxson was emotionally absent from their relationship during Cory's formative years. In the seven-year time period covered by the play, Cory remains resentful; even as he begins to understand the challenges and choices his baseball player-turned-garbage collector father faced over the years.

I dove wholeheartedly into our performances of George C. Wolfe's *Colored Museum*—a series of eleven vignettes satirizing elements of African American culture and designed to bring the viewing audience into the production as a participant. My favorite of the many characters I played in the production was Miss Roj, an outspoken drag queen who relays the pain of homophobia and racial discrimination in, "The Gospel According to Miss Roj." The production team dressed me up in a cutoff tank top, women's jewelry, and garish makeup for the role.

"God created black people, and black people created style. The name is Miss Roj. That's R-o-j. You can find me here every, Wednesday, Friday, and Saturday nights here at the Bottomless Pit. The watering hole for the wild, and weary!"

I snapped my fingers and swayed my hips wide as I walked, laying down Miss Roj's beats. "Snap for every time you walk past someone homeless on the street smelling like piss and shit, and you act like you don't even see it. Each snap puts you one step closer to the end," I warned the audience. "Snap your fingers and dance!" All of my football teammates who came out to see the show wasted no time making Miss Roj a bit of a celebrity among the entire team.

But I didn't mind. My work with the BTE—which had between fifteen and twenty active members at any time—was adding to my résumé of responsibility. The outgoing president was so impressed by my participation and passion, he asked me to serve for the 1996-1997 school year.

I was truly happy for the first time in my life. Overworked and exhausted, but delighted with my new life as The Hustle Man. I had survived and moved on to thrive. The darkness of my youth passed and I was racing toward the bright lights of my future.

Or so I thought.

* * * * * * * * *

As soon as I saw the men in suits coming down the aisle, there was no doubt in my mind they were coming for me and it had something to do with my former life. The professor looked up from the podium and every head in the place watched their progression. I was in a biology lecture with about three hundred other students, sitting in the section of seats on the left side of the hall. They walked straight over to where I was seated.

"Are you Robert Singleton?" asked a man, who despite his loose dress shirt was built like a linebacker. I wasn't even shocked. I did wonder for a few seconds how they knew which student I was, but figured they must have asked someone out in the hall or the back of the room to point me out before they came in. "You need to come with us."

I grabbed my books and followed them up the stairs to the exit. They stopped and put a pair of handcuffs on me. "You're under arrest for murder," one leaned in and informed me. I waited for them to read me my rights.

Immediately I started thinking back to my time in Perry Homes—any and all scraps I had gotten mixed up in and whether any of them would have garnered me a murder charge. My conscience was clear. I'd messed around on the streets a bit, but none of my actions had resulted in something as serious as murder.

We exited the building and they led me over to sit on a bench. A third man joined us. I recognized him from Perry Homes and understood immediately he'd been an undercover cop. He started talking, asking if I knew the whereabouts of my cousin Carlos and what he'd been up to the last few years. When I admitted I had no idea, he informed me Carlos had used my identity when arrested by the police. He had my driver's license information and I had no record, so the cops didn't immediately realize they'd been scammed. The officer said my license had been suspended for some time now as they searched for me.

I let his words wash over me. *Okay, God,* I thought looking down at the thick green grass below my feet, *if it's your will for me to do ten or fifteen years for a crime I didn't commit, so be it. It's your plan.*

The man who'd first spoken in the lecture hall walked behind me and reached for my arms. I figured he was about to yank me up and toss me in a patrol car. He unlocked the handcuffs and removed them without a word.

"You can go back to class if you want to," the undercover officer told me. He stood and walked away with the other Georgia Bureau of Investigation men.

As soon as they started their car and pulled away, I sprinted for home. There was no way I was going back into the lecture hall after being humiliated in front of my peers. I'd have to face their questions eventually, but not today. A quick call to 579 Clarissa let them know what was going on and launched what would be a several-year process of removing the file recording "my" arrest and clearing my record. Things really had changed, I realized when I hung up the phone. There was no desire to run, scream, or rage, and I felt no real frustration from the situation. *Guess that's what it means to be a grownup*. There was no fear, no doubt. I knew everything would work out okay if I maintained my trust in God and whatever plan He had for me; if I kept following my path with truth and love in my heart. I promised myself, whatever came I would do just that.

Chapter 21
Reflections

The mirror never lied. No matter how many times I stood in front of it, the mirror always told me the truth of my condition. The truth was in the eyes. The mirror in the Performance Studio at the Department of Theatre & Film Studies covered an entire wall. The room was a favorite of mine—the site of my first acting classes at UGA, nestled on the ground floor near the Cellar Theatre just below the larger Fine Arts Theatre.

I was supposed to be practicing lines for our latest production, *In the Time of the Revolution*, in which I was set to play several characters including Victor Hugo. Instead, I just stared. The man in the mirror looked so different from the child who gazed—half-crazed with frustration—in a much smaller reflective glass in the bathroom at 579 Clarissa. I was bigger, with broad shoulders and thick thighs from all of my football weight training. My acne was clearing up. The face looking back at me flashed a broad smile. But the changes in the mirror weren't just physical. I was bigger emotionally, hardened by the knocks I'd taken early on, but stronger because of them. I had learned to take responsibility. Not a burden I couldn't lift, but a source of pride knowing I could manage anything that came across my path. I stared hard. This mirror was bigger, I could see more detail, and I looked for signs of disquiet in the man staring back at me. What I saw was a man who knew the course he was on and was content at the moment.

* * * * * * * * *

The Cellar Theatre was not the UGA theatre program's premier venue, but it was my favorite. Perhaps because many of the productions I acted in during my time at the university—including

Six in a Flat and *Chamber Music*—were before the intimate audiences of a hundred or so people sitting snugly in the theatre's limited demi-circle seating. The theatre was longer than it was wide, with the audience seating, stage, and backstage area interlinked like the cars of a child's train set. It had no windows, creating a full immersion experience for the audience.

Playing the lead in Carlyle Brown's *The African Company Presents Richard III*—James Hewlett—was one of my proudest moments in that theatre. The play is based on the real-world travails of America's first-recorded black performing troupe in New York City during the 1820s. The troupe, run by William Henry Brown, was trying to perform *Richard III* in 1821, angering a rival white troupe manager. Hired hecklers beset them repeatedly; they faced allegations of fire code violations, and finally police constables looking to shut the production down.

Actor James Hewlett had played Richard III, and I was playing Hewlett—who, alongside the rest of the troupe, was pulled from the stage and arrested. Taking the risk to set an example of what is right—as the people of The African Company did—made sense to me. Their brave actions were the kind I wished I had been exposed to in my younger years, and exemplified the type of determination I wanted my young daughter to see as she grew. Even if it would be quite a few years before she would do more than sleep through my performances.

Commaleta and I had a crazy schedule going. I handed Commaleta the baby before my classes and then switched with her during her psychology classes. When it was time for football practice, Commaleta took the baby back until it was time to go to work. I'd bring Heavven with me to rehearsals at the theater department. Right from the start, Heavven was a trouper. She took a bottle and sat there pretty quiet while we ran lines. Most of the time, she'd fall asleep and was good for about two hours. But when she didn't, other actors who weren't in the scene being rehearsed would rock her or play with her to keep her quiet. At random intervals, Heavven would squeal happily. We usually took that to mean we were doing a good job.

* * * * * * * * *

Hard work and progress rarely come without challenges, and Commaleta and I had our share. One of my biggest challenges came during a football practice in the spring of my junior year.

The sports medicine team took excellent care of me, scheduling ultrasound and other therapies three times a day to help me recover from a torn ligament in my ankle. I was already somewhat frustrated by my progress in my football career. I was just as good and working just as hard as many of my peers before the injury temporarily sidelined me. But I wasn't getting playing time during games as it was, being on the scout team. With an injury, the chances I'd have to make any sort of impression for a shot at the draft were dissipating by the day. I continued to play, but in my heart I knew my dreams of making it as a professional football player were fading.

In the end, I only played in one football game as a Bulldog. It was the Outback Bowl against Wisconsin down in Tampa Bay on January 1, 1998, during my senior year. I went out on the field with the confidence I'd always displayed in practice. I wasn't nervous and joked with my teammates as they began to shout. After years of waiting, I finally got my shot at playing division one ball in a Bowl game.

"Aw yeah! Hustle Man's in the game. You gotta do it to 'em, Hustle, take it to 'em good!"

"A'right, a'right. Which one you want me to do?"

I stepped up to the line and took aim at the player my teammates pointed out. "Sorry, man, I gotta destroy you," I taunted as we waited for the snap.

The ball ended up going to a different player and my target took off in another direction, denying me contact. We blew Wisconsin out in the game, thirty-three to six at the final whistle. It was the only play I made in a Georgia Bulldog game.

As my time with the Bulldogs wound down and I watched professional football teams pick up my teammates, I knew there was so much more I could have done. I worked hard, and couldn't believe God brought me out of the projects to warm benches at the University of Georgia only to fade away after. It wasn't easy to reconcile. The one thing I had clung to as the foundation for a successful future wasn't the long-term path I was meant to travel. I made the decision to place my faith, as I had so many times before, in the belief He wanted more from me. Football had served its purpose in my life and it was time to move on. I gave thanks for the years of lessons, discipline, and growth football had afforded me.

By the time we packed up our apartment on Church Street and drove away for the last time in the Ford, I had already turned my attention to acting full-time.

Chapter 22
The Vow

I turned my head to the right and looked over at the beautiful woman standing next to me. She had no frills or fancy makeup; just a diamond polished by the rough and tumble of being kicked 'round the streets a bit. A natural beauty. For years I had known she was what I wanted, even when she pushed me off. She had been right to make me wait.

But as I gazed at Commaleta—three months pregnant with our second child Nevvaeh, wearing a loose gray shirt and comfortable shoes—and waited for the judge to do his part, I knew we were both finally ready to cement our relationship and begin a real life together as man and wife.

* * * * * * * * *

We moved into 2109 Gladeview in a Stone Mountain, GA apartment complex called Timber Trace shortly after leaving UGA. It was a middle-class neighborhood, at least to us. We had a two-bedroom ground-floor apartment with about eight hundred square feet for seven hundred and fifty-five dollars a month. The apartment had extra wide hallways and bathroom—built as a residence for handicapped individuals. We took it because it was the only open unit the complex had available when we wanted to move in. It took everything we had to keep Heavven from racing between the bedrooms and the living room on her Big Wheel. We'd send her to the hilly courtyard outside for her vehicular activities in a bid to save the apartment walls. And our sanity.

From the outside we may have looked like a cohesive family unit, but the truth was we were falling apart. We were trying hard to keep the peace since our move from Church Street, where I spent the last few weeks orchestrating arguments intended to drive a wedge between us and further conceal my infidelities. The graphic words we exchanged were laced with vulgar insults flying between the two of us with the precision of stealth missiles.

The tension between us reached its peak one night when we packed up our fragile family and overnight bags to pay a holiday visit to family and friends in Atlanta for the New Year. While stopping at a Taco Bell for dinner on the way, an argument erupted over a simple disagreement about which of us was the better driver. There had been many verbal tirades before but this one in particular took us to a crossroad that forced us to question our love, our principles, and our desire to continue. I tossed Commaleta's food on her lap out of frustration. It provoked a violent chain reaction.

I sat in the driver's seat of our newly acquired vehicle in the restaurant parking lot staring at Commaleta in disbelief, my face covered in the contents of a taco supreme she had just lobbed at me. The sour cream and lettuce clung to the side of my face, the shell and remaining contents splattered over my chest and stomach. I'd never contemplated laying my hands on a woman, especially not the woman I loved more than any other, but my instinct to retaliate boiled inside me like hot lava. With our eight-month old daughter sitting calmly in the back as a dark storm loomed within the confines of the now-foggy windows of our Nissan Altima, I decided now was not the time to seek vengeance.

I trembled with anger, and drove silently back in the direction of our small apartment. The road-trip was off. And "it" was on. I'm sure Commaleta sensed my level of tension, she too maintained a stony silence. When we arrived home and Heavven was safely out of view of my next premeditated retort, I took my shot. I speared the paper cup of soda and ice from my value meal toward Commaleta, striking her in the chest just above her breast. Though it truly wasn't my intention to hurt anything more than her feelings by drenching her with diluted syrup, the bottom corner of the cup hit her at the worst possible angle in an area delicate enough to cause a lot of pain. After a slight pause to process the pain and the shock of my actions, Commaleta rushed me, fists in a knot, lower lip hanging low. She huffed and puffed with a rage I had never seen in her and didn't know existed in her five-feet-four inches tall, one hundred thirty pound petite frame; someone I had known to be so delicate, mild-mannered, and loving. If things were not so heated, it would have been a sight cute enough for gut-busting laughter. I stood long enough to allow her to push me and kick me in the shin before backing and turning away to end the standoff, knowing I had been the one to cross a line defined by us both—the one establishing us as a non-physically abusive couple. A line setting us apart from the domestic abuse we'd both witnessed way too often as kids. Like Cat, Commaleta's mother had been in and out of physically abusive relationships. Our commitment to avoid interrelationship violence was part of what defined us as a couple. I had unleashed the worst in us both and knew our relationship faced a horrible truth. Our respect for each other was shattered and our hopes for sustaining the relationship seemed far out of reach.

By the time we moved to Stone Mountain, Commaleta's frustration with my relative lack of commitment to the family— even though I was holding down a job and providing for our basic needs—boiled over. I was frustrated by her insistence on challenging my decisions and actions. For some reason, I still believed she didn't need to know where I was or what I was doing as long as I eventually came home.

We decided to separate once again while we still shared living space in the apartment.

It worked for me ... at first, anyway. Commaleta hadn't found suitable employment yet, so it was easy to convince her staying in the apartment, despite our estrangement, was the best thing for Heavven. Commaleta made blind, hopeful, cold calls to convince would-be homeowners to participate in an accelerated biweekly mortgage program—the first in a series of failed business ventures we would try. We didn't have the money to own a home yet, but once we attended the program's two-hour seminar, we were convinced it was a good opportunity. After months of phone calls, house calls, and online marketing efforts resulted in only a single prospect, Commaleta was practically housebound by financial circumstances and the need to care for our daughter, even as I ventured out to hang with friends and talk to other women. A couple weeks into the separation, I suggested in addition to continuing to share a living space, we should still share a bed. I had learned long before, Commaleta might not be street tough, but she had an extremely strong backbone and a level of self-respect that made her regard my request with sheer disdain.

She had made the decision during the second half of our senior year of high school on her eighteenth birthday to finally give herself completely to me in the physical sense. It was partly because of anger and frustration that spawned from a recent argument with her mother—a fight that left her emotionally drained and with a strong desire for my embrace—but also because of our enduring love for one another and the years I'd dedicated to our relationship without forcing the issue of sex. I had been with many girls and women, but that day after school in the bedroom at 579 surrounded by walls that had witnessed so much pain and impurity, I would experience passionate lovemaking for the first time. And Commaleta would lose her virginity to someone she expected to be with for eternity.

My lascivious proposition all these years later was like daggers to the heart as she scanned my face for the slightest hint of humor. She concluded her decision to give herself to me so many years ago outside of marriage had been a foolish choice, even though it had ultimately led to the birth of the beautiful baby girl we equally loved and adored.

My idea to firmly establish my dominant position in the relationship by resuming sexual relations to hopefully bring her in line, backfired on me.

Just a couple of months after moving into the place at Timber Trace, Commaleta was out the door to live with her mother, taking our daughter with her.

I visited my daughter every chance I got. Commaleta was distant, but polite, rebuffing any attempt I made to reignite our flame.

"You love your daughter, and that's all there is," she said on more than one occasion.

But I caught her watching me when I played with Heavven. Sometimes she looked hurt, most of the time she just looked disappointed—pursing her lips and shaking her head like she could somehow erase the reality of our situation and make it better. Her silent admonitions embarrassed and angered me. As much as I wanted to be with her, she needed to understand the power dynamic of our relationship.

Despite the drastically different ways in which we viewed the situation, we both experienced our breaking point on the very same day.

Commaleta was checking her appearance in the mirror, adding dabs of makeup when I showed up to talk to her minutes before she would head out for her first day as an administrative assistant for Xerox.

"You may want to get yourself tested."

She swayed as if my words had been a physical hit. A small part of me was angry I had to admit to contracting a mild sexually transmitted disease, urethritis, from a one-night stand back at UGA. The overwhelming feeling in my gut as I explained the problem to her was shame.

Up until then, Commaleta had no idea I'd had sexual relations with other women, that off-and-on for years I had been unfaithful. But it was the way men acted, wasn't it? In the 'hood if you only had one girl, you were a punk. My refusal to allow my peers to brand me as such resulted in my wholehearted embrace of their warped philosophy. Somehow what started as a childlike exploration of sexuality evolved into habitual, egotistical, and delusional acts of overcompensation. My thinking was poor, uneducated, ignorant, oppressed. I lacked the necessary essentials to claim true manhood and instead engaged in superficial expressions of adult behavior. I cussed, bragged, cuffed my crotch, and had meaningless sex in a bid to assert my manhood and further my understanding of my humanity.

The second part of the dysfunctional philosophy on behavior also dictated, ironically—you never let your main girl catch you in the act. Even though our recent conversations revealed I was talking to other women, I had never before given any hint that I was pursuing sexual relations with anyone other than her. Now it was all coming out into the open. I watched a host of emotions cross her face. Confusion. Denial. Anger. Disgust. Pain.

"Well congratulations, Rob, you did it. You pulled one right over on me." Her voice shook. I knew her too well to think tears would follow. I could practically feel her steeling herself to make a stand. "I was so gullible, just a naive fool." She walked back and forth across the room thinking.

"What do you want from me?" Her voice grew stronger with each word. She turned to face me straight on and without giving me a chance to respond continued. "You want me to tell you this is okay? Because it's not. It's so far from okay it's on another planet." Commaleta was torn up by the reality of my betrayal, but also shocked by the level of discretion with which I'd conducted myself.

I struggled to defend my actions as the realization hit; I had once again critically wounded one of the people who meant the most to me in this world. For all my talk of love and respect after the taco debacle, I had disrespected the woman I loved. I did what I could to manage the paradox unfolding in my mind. The remorse I felt for what I had done wasn't enough to prevent me from doing it in the first place.

The journey to real adulthood that began when my mother passed away was leading me to a spiritual crossroads of possible redemption. I wanted it so badly I could taste it. To be the kind of man who aspires to make a positive impact. But my actions were far from fulfilling my wish.

Commaleta listened as I fumbled through an explanation, but I could tell by the way she continued to get ready for work, she was immediately dismissing the words the moment they left my lips.

"I don't know if we can fix this." She opened the door to usher me out of her mother's place. "I don't know if I even want to try."

Her disposition toward me changed. In the weeks following, Commaleta's manner was akin to a military drill sergeant more than a wounded woman facing the threat of being a single mother. She was straightforward and rigid in her discussions with me, posing rational arguments devoid of emotion. It hit me; she was at the point of being done with me. I was losing my family.

My sole focus became to change my behavior and regain what I had lost. It was bad enough I had grown up in a broken home with well-meaning relatives doing their best to fill in the gaps where a mother and father should be. I would not let it happen to my daughter. I would be there to nurture and support her, to hold her hand if she felt the need to rage in front of a bathroom mirror. Commaleta was a wonderful mother, equal parts love and discipline. An added bonus to a truth I had known for a long time but didn't understand—she was the one I wanted to spend my life with, to make more babies with.

As part of my quest to right my wrongs, I decided to leave Timber Trace, move back to my grandparents' place, and hand the keys to the apartment over to Commaleta. It was the right thing to do as Commaleta was the primary caretaker of our daughter and Heavven deserved her own space to run and play. Commaleta was also thriving at her new job and now able to stand on her own financially.

I continued to visit Heavven as often as I could, doing my best to explain my changed mindset to Commaleta. Explained how I understood where my duty lay, and how to live up to the responsibility. I understood her mistrust and obvious reluctance to believe me, and couldn't get angry no matter how much I despised the situation. I prayed on it. Hoped Commaleta would somehow see I was being truthful. Months and months of work later, I was rewarded when she finally agreed to sit down and talk with me about where we were.

She had been going to clubs on occasion with friends. The grinding and sexing against the walls of a dance club brought home how much she valued being involved with someone committed to the journey of a long-term relationship. I said a quick prayer of thanks for the lustful individuals who helped bring my love back to the table. We both had expectations and we took great pains to relay them clearly. Giving our love another shot meant approaching it with open lines of communication and sense of internal equality within the relationship.

Our apartment at Timber Trace teemed with the sounds of life once she opened the door for me to return home in the spring of 1999. It had been a tumultuous year, one neither of us would soon forget. We were still nursing our wounds, but we were stronger for the tribulation.

Although Commaleta wanted to wait until we were married to resume the sexual part of our relationship, I managed to wear her down. Three months later, she was pregnant.

* * * * * * * * *

The decision to marry came so naturally there was no doubt it was the right course. We were driving on Memorial Drive, coming back from Athens, GA and stopped at a few jewelry stores to view wedding rings along the way. It sparked renewed talk of marriage, family, and the future. We decided right then to get married. Neither Commaleta nor I had any real interest in a big wedding. We were both twenty-four and on our way to being parents for the second time. It was the tenth of December 1999, and the time was finally right.

We went to the DeKalb County Courthouse eager to get in line and processed before they closed at midnight. Apparently we were the only ones looking to get married this particular night and sat in the waiting area alone. When they called our names, we rose and walked into the chamber holding hands to face the judge, ready to recite our vows.

Chapter 23
Acting Secrets

Baltimore, Orlando, Jacksonville, Kalamazoo, and Cleveland. I was on my way, literally. Every time I thought about it, my situation made me giggle a little bit. On the street, a sugar daddy was slang for a guy, usually older, who provides for women of his choosing—apartments, money, chocolate, jewelry—in exchange for companionship. For me, I was convinced *Sugar Daddy* was it— the big break.

In early 2000, I traveled around the country, performing on stage with renowned entertainers such as New Edition's Ralph Tresvant, Ali Woodson (R.I.P.) from the Temptations, Bernadette Stanis (Thelma) from *Good Times* and Christopher Martin (Play) from Kid 'N' Play. We performed eight shows a week—twice on Saturday and Sundays so we could all have Mondays off—in theaters filled with appreciative crowds. I was earning eight hundred dollars a week for my efforts, a good paycheck for an upcoming actor from Atlanta.

It was a major step forward from my first feature film gig, a featured extra role in the Denzel Washington football and racial integration film, *Remember the Titans*. I wasn't a lead in this production of *Sugar Daddy* either, but I was playing several roles— one of them as the "boy toy" to Bernadette Stanis' character.

In less than two years after graduating, I was sharing stage and screen time with entertainers I'd idolized as a child. Actors I watched and admired growing up—successful well-balanced individuals I hoped to emulate when I began to act myself. Denzel Washington took the time to come on to the bus during the filming of *Remember the Titans* to talk to the young men playing members of the Titans football team. He spoke of perseverance, respect, and pride in accomplishment. His definition of success, as

I recall, was not measured by looking at where you found yourself in life, but the acknowledgement of where you began and what it took to get there, and then setting the bar higher still. I didn't have much at the time, but his words made me feel like I was already a success. In a strange, but not all-together surprising way, he sounded a lot like the character—Coach Herman Boone—he portrayed in the film. He inspired me to take a somewhat critical look at the projects I was considering, to aim for selecting productions that examined the human condition in a way that promoted truth and love.

Those two qualities went hand-in-hand with generosity of spirit. Even though she was pregnant with our second child, Commaleta bade me to take my shot. Like me, she felt *Sugar Daddy* was an important milestone for my acting career, so I hit the road and came back home just a few weeks before our second daughter, Nevvaeh, joined this world on June twenty-seventh.

Being on the road, even for the relatively short run of *Sugar Daddy*, left me energized, ready for the next project. For the next several months my most important project involved a lot of diapers and onesies. Every chance I got; I'd lay with her in my arms and assure Nevvaeh I was working hard for our family. Nevvaeh was just beginning to crawl around after her big sister Heavven by the time I moved on to my next project, *Secrets*.

* * * * * * * * *

Secrets scared me. They scared Eddie too. I played Eddie, a high school football player in his senior year being recruited to play college ball. He'd engaged in sexual activity and subsequently heard about HIV/AIDS at school. Eddie headed for a testing center, telling the audience the troubling truth that drove him there.

"A person can look completely healthy and still have the virus. But I'm not going to die, I've got a full scholarship to college next year," he insisted as he waited for test results. "Five years ago, I didn't know what AIDS meant ... in some ways I still don't."

Every time I said the line, I knew exactly what Eddie meant.

The production—aimed at raising awareness about HIV/AIDS, was sponsored by Kaiser Permanente—required all of the cast members, three men and two women, to get tested before the show's premiere performance. We were already in rehearsal when I went in to have my test.

With my history of sexual activity and Momma Cat's death, I was scared out of my wits. I was getting a small taste of the fear Momma Cat must have experienced in her battle against the disease and the fear was pretty close to debilitating. The mere thought something invisible, incurable, and deadly, could be coursing silently through my veins left me light-headed and nauseous.

Secrets had a minimalist approach to set design. We used boxes about the size of college dorm refrigerators as our only real props. We shifted them around the stage while we performed, to serve as chairs, a dance floor, or a girl's bedroom depending on the scene.

Eddie, a girl he asked out named Monica, a doctor, and a hotline counselor were among the characters relaying their experiences and information about HIV/AIDS. We performed *Secrets* at high schools and community centers around Atlanta from the fall of 2000 through spring 2001, working to raise awareness of the ways the disease could be contracted and prevention techniques, ways individuals could get tested, and access support services to cope with it.

At the end of each performance, we would open the floor for discussion. Over a decade into the AIDS pandemic people still had plenty of questions. HIV/AIDS had decimated low-economic communities across the United States because of a lack of awareness, distrust of the system, and a lack of access to appropriate treatment. People living in middle or upper-class neighborhoods were more likely to know about the disease and receive treatment than poorer folk. The 1985 disclosure that Rock Hudson had AIDS was followed by a string of similar celebrity cases. Freddie Mercury. Magic Johnson. Arthur Ashe. Mass public awareness campaigns, including commercials, sex education in schools, and theater productions ranging from *Secrets* to *And the Band Played On* dominated mainstream American culture in the 1990s. Yet still the questions, fear, and doubts continued. After each *Secrets* performance, I prayed the message had not only been heard, but understood—that out there among the audience leaving the theater, there were individuals who would take steps to protect themselves. Those who would escape the fate Momma Cat and millions of others around the world had suffered, and give love and support to those afflicted by the deadly disease.

In *Secrets*, when Eddie's number at the testing center is called, the doctors inform him he is HIV positive and he agonizes over their recommendation he seek out counseling.

"So I can sit around talking about how I'm dying before I can even graduate."

I was far more fortunate than Eddie. My test results were negative. To this day, HIV/AIDS remains among one of the leading killers of African American males and other population groups. It remains a global plague.

Chapter 24
On My Way

I'd steered the Mazda Milennia through Birmingham, Jackson, and Shreveport, and on to Dallas before taking anything longer than a quick restroom, food grab, or roadside nap stop. Views of the majestic country I drove through kept me entertained during the daylight hours. I found myself in awe of the vast land unfolding around me. I became lost in thought as the echoes of the land's history rippled through a frigid winter air. Each gust of wind seemed to carry a piece of the past with it. The actions of defiant forty-two-year-old civil rights activist Rosa Parks, Martin Luther King Jr.'s incarceration in Birmingham for a rights campaign, and the determination of 1960s Governor George Wallace to champion "segregation forever" in Montgomery, rode with me through Alabama. The rifle shot that ended civil rights activist Medgar Evers' efforts to help integrate the University of Mississippi accompanied me in that state. Through Texas, I traveled with the memory of men who held strong and died at the Alamo to defend the idea of freedom, and remembered where a charismatic rights advocate and president lost his life around lunchtime on a sunny November day in 1963.

The pain of 9-11 was still fresh. In the wake of the devastating September eleventh attacks on New York and Washington, D.C., I struggled to understand how any man, from any cultural, political, or religious background, could justify taking the lives of thousands of men, women, and children. Every life is a gift, a precious blessing. Decade after decade the world witnessed horrifying assaults defying common logic, but the assaults persisted. 9-11 was just the latest on a long list of grisly examples. The loss made my heart ache.

At night the only thing I saw in the headlights was the highway stretching out before me. I kept the window open and the music turned up, singing along with each song I recognized. Amarillo, Albuquerque, Flagstaff. Signs with the cities' names and mile markers materialized out of the dark at my car's headlights approach. The passing of each brought me closer to my final destination—Los Angeles, CA. Every time I passed the sign of a city I recognized, I thanked God for walking beside me on this path, and mentally prepared for the success I was sure to find in Hollywood.

I raced toward my future and drove cross-country as quickly as any human could expect to. The sooner I arrived, the sooner I'd make my mark. In the months following the end of *Secrets*, it became clear I was falling behind on my personal goals with the acting work available in the Atlanta area. I'd thought Hollywood would know my name within a year of leaving UGA. Three years later, there was no doubt in my mind; I needed to do more to achieve my goal. It's great to talk about being successful and dream about how it will happen, but terrible to sit around and wait for it. I was ready. I just had to get the opportunity ... and I was determined to make it happen.

The only contact I had in Los Angeles was through a friend of my mother-in-law, but I wasn't worried as I planned my trip westward. I had confidence and talent; when combined with my drive and discipline, I would get results in Tinseltown.

Forged in the burning heat of Perry Homes' streets, I was sturdy, strong, and ready to build the foundation for a successful life for my family. But it was more than that. I had confidence in my spirit. By forging ahead on a path marked with truth and love, I would use my natural talent not only to succeed for myself, but also create hope for my family and others. Help them believe the dreams they had could be real. I would find my way and soar, counting on my faith in God and His message to help keep me on course. I would succeed for myself, but also my children, my wife ... for Tracy, Momzie, and Big Larry. And Momma Cat.

My thought process on progress gave birth to a refined identity. I was, and always would be Robert, but I had grown into so much more. My trials in life had forged me into IronE—strong, solid and unbreakable like the metal, but with a spirit carrying me upward on my journey, raising me above the trials that had come before. With an ironclad and steadfast determination to succeed, I could accomplish anything. "An eagle in flight with an unbroken spirit," would be my guiding theme as IronE. Electrifying, energetic, enigmatic, enlightened, empowered. I could be whatever I wanted to be. I was soaring upward and onward, far beyond the physical and mental limitations socialization, environment, genetics, stereotypes, statistics, and history had placed on me. The irony that a "nobody" from "nowhere" could defy the odds and do what no one in my family had done before? The pundits might say, "Never! No way! No how!" But I would respectfully disagree. I was IronE. I hoped the name would also help crack the ice and drive interest, give me the opportunity to tell my story in the hopes of inspiring other would-be IronE's in the world.

With a renewed sense of purpose, I packed up the car and started driving on the first of February 2002, knowing the future was right ahead of me.

* * * * * * * * *

I hit Hollywood ground running—or rather, standing—arriving in Los Angeles on a Thursday afternoon with just enough time to grab a few hours of sleep and get in line at a cattle call for ABC in Burbank. It was the beginning of pilot season. The time of year when Hollywood kicks into high gear, auditioning actors for productions slated to debut later in the year on all the networks. ABC was looking to cast actors for a showcase and perhaps select a handful to go on to their fall shows. After eight hours of waiting with hundreds of others, I was near the front of the line when a lady in a suit came out to inform us they were done for the day.

"Sorry, you guys. You're going to have to come back on Monday," she said as people around me began to express their frustrations. She had a friendly enough face, and her tone was kind, but for a few seconds I had the urge to grab her by the shoulders and start shaking. I was a little surprised by my reaction. I'm usually a pretty patient guy.

I took a couple deep breaths to calm myself. "May I have a ticket or something, so I can keep my place in line?"

"No you have to start over. You may want to make sure you get here earlier."

I did my best to conceal my frustration, kindly thanked her, and walked away to get in my car, where I proceeded to scream. I sincerely hoped, afterward, that no one had seen the outburst.

I spent the weekend reminding myself, anything worth having took hard work and determination. I needed to be patient and wait for my chance to walk through the door. Driving at a breakneck pace across the country had only been one leg on this stretch of my journey. I needed to keep showing up, add to my investment in my future. Monday morning I arrived at the audition location over an hour before the call was set to open, and spent another three hours waiting to take my first shot at Hollywood. I made it in the door and had what I thought was a solid showing.

With the sheer volume of people who had shown up to audition, I wasn't sure I would get a callback, and even if I did, a callback didn't ensure I'd book the gig.

I set about getting my L.A. life in order while I waited. The first step was to reach out to my mother-in-law's friend's cousin who owned a restaurant on La Tijera Boulevard, and secure temporary employment until I started booking acting jobs. I launched the search for a place to live, looking for a living situation with roommates to help manage my expenditures, and began preparing a list of L.A.-based agents to send my résumé and headshot.

When the callback from the cattle call came, I knew I was on my way. A callback is a second round of auditions; a kind of validation of the work an actor put in and an acknowledgement the production team sees possibilities. I went to the callback bursting with confidence, grateful I'd made the cut on my first shot after having just arrived in L.A. and auditioning against so many other actors equally hungry for a job. The second round of auditions was at ABC studios, reading a script from Michael J. Fox's sitcom *Spin City*.

As I left the studios, I knew I had nailed it and figured I wouldn't be working at the restaurant for long. I was only half-right.

Chapter 25
Headshots

When I wasn't at work at the restaurant the Townhouse, or at my second job at a Cajun place La Louisianne, I relentlessly pursued my Hollywood dream. I didn't get the nickname Hustle Man for nothing. I made calls, trying to set up meetings or internships in the industry. After I finished phone calls for the day, I'd spend hours on the small assembly line of envelopes, stamps, résumés, and headshots I'd fashioned on top of the small desk in the bedroom I was sharing with a roommate.

Over the course of my first few weeks in L.A., I sent out over a hundred headshots and résumés to theatrical agents and casting companies, fully expecting to hear back from several interested parties. Weeks passed and each trip to the mailbox failed to produce any responses. There had been no further follow-up call from the ABC auditions. Each day that passed, the chances for an opportunity to be picked up for one of the pilots faded.

I expressed my frustrations over the phone to Commaleta, grateful for her continuing support and her belief in my talent. She encouraged me to be patient and keep working toward my goal. "You keep on walking your path, Singie," she urged. "Your time will come."

When the letter arrived, I hesitated before opening it. The return address was CAA, Creative Artists Agency, one of the biggest agencies in the business. I stared at the print, which jiggled a little thanks to a slight shaking of my hands which began as soon as I noticed the name. It was the only response I'd gotten thus far, or would get—and it wasn't the letter I expected. CAA could not consider me for representation because I was not a member of the Screen Actors Guild. Most actors in the industry are members of SAG—a labor union formed in 1933 to protect the interests of working performers. I placed the letter on the bedroom desk in plain view, so I would be continuously reminded that walking the path is a learning experience and got ready for my next shift at the Cajun restaurant.

* * * * * * * * *

I was waiting tables the day Michael Colyar—who had been on the television show *Martin* and would later lend his voice talent to *The Princess and the Frog*—finally agreed to give me a shot at the crowd during the Townhouse's comedy night. I was nervous, but ready, as I took off my apron and left it in the break room. When I headed to the stage, I was too wrapped up in thoughts of Colyar calling to the crowd to welcome IronE Singleton to feel the butterflies swarming in my stomach. I was still getting used to hearing the name and in the beginning process of understanding what it meant to live up to the moniker I'd adopted. It was the first time I'd ever heard it announced to a crowd. I had nothing to worry about, I thought, I had my routine down pat. Hours of practice in the bedroom mirror were about to pay off.

I'd only managed to tell two jokes before some faceless member of the crowd let out a loud, "Boo!" Keeping a smile on my face and pushing forward with my set was a Herculean effort in gag reflex control. My stomach squirmed with nerves and pushed my lunch up the back of my throat. For a moment, I considered dashing off the stage for the exit over by the hostess station. I was a little surprised by my reaction. This wasn't the first time I had been on stage. Nor was it the first time I'd encountered an unruly crowd. But this was L.A., and if I bombed word might spread and end my career before it really got started. I could dance, act, rap … and now my dreams were going to end right there. *I'm doomed … I'll never work in this town again*, I thought as I fought to keep my composure. *Their scorn is going to send me off the stage into oblivion.*

By the time I got to my fourth joke, there was more derision than laughter rolling my way from the restaurant floor. Colyar, the guy who headlined Thursday's "Open Mic" comedy show, jumped on stage to play along with the unruly crowd and buried me deeper than they had. I just stood there, staring at him, feeling the heat of embarrassment stinging my cheeks. How had things gone so wrong, so quickly?

Colyar came to find me when it was over. He seemed to genuinely want me to understand that his mini-roast on the stage really wasn't anything personal. It was all a part of making sure the audience had a good show. It was performance theater in its most basic and intimate form. My joke about September eleventh and the Twin Towers attack was too soon to be funny, he told me. I shook my head and asked him how he could say that, we'd both seen other comedians do jokes related to the terrorist attacks on New York and Washington and get good responses. My problem had been my timing and delivery, I knew it. He didn't disagree. Colyar encouraged me to keep working at my routine and refine my approach to the career goals I'd set. As he walked away, I felt disheartened and a little confused. I wasn't quite sure what I was supposed to do next, but I knew for sure I wouldn't get back up on that particular stage again. I wasn't as ready as I'd thought.

* * * * * * * * *

Even with working two jobs and sharing a cramped two-bedroom apartment with two roommates and a toddler, I was using my credit cards to get by. Part of my salary went back home to help Commaleta manage living expenses for her and the kids. She had recently landed a job with the Georgia Professional Standards Commission (PSC) as a database coordinator. Her job helped us make up some of the budget shortfalls coming as a result of our family being divided up on two coasts. Headshot printing costs, four-dollar-a-gallon gas, wardrobe for auditions, and a four hundred dollar car repair bill right after I'd arrived kept taking chunks out of my available credit.

As pilot season ended, the only things I had to show for weeks of hard work were one callback, a refusal letter, credit card debt, burns from carrying hot dinner plates, and the echoes of a crowd booing me off a stage. My living situation was uncomfortable at best; splitting a bedroom with a guy I barely knew, whose militant religious outlook and blatant racism was in direct conflict with my beliefs.

He was a militant Muslim. Every other word he said seemed to be "cracka'" this and "cracka" that. I felt it was safe to assume he was holding a slight grudge against the white man for past transgressions. *Oh God, why me*, I thought on several occasions. Then it dawned on me; God presented me with the situation for a reason. Things weren't really as terrible as I had initially thought once I altered my perspective. It was an opportunity for me to teach—to enlighten. I used every waking moment I was around him to convey to him, race—like religion and politics—was a man-made construct devised to keep people of different "groups" at odds with one another.

"How are there different races if we all come from the same source? How are there different races if the source that created me and you also created every Becky, Pedro, Luisa, Shaneeka, Wang, Peter, Red Cloud, and Leroy?" Another time I adopted a different tone. "It's evident in the fact that we're all made of the same thing underneath our variant hues and texture of skin and hair. At our core we are all the same."

What I said seemed to provide him with a different kind of approach than he'd ever heard, probably because he'd been around similarly thinking people. The biggest clue he'd absorbed what I'd said was a noticeable decrease in use of his favorite word, cracka.

It wasn't the first time I'd had an experience give me pause, make me wonder how in the twenty-first century such thinking could persist. My previous encounter was with a cop when I was exiting a movie theater on the outskirts of Atlanta. He accused me of entering theaters without paying and told me a lot of white people wished black people still had few rights so they could enjoy their outings in peace. I suspected he was one of the white people he mentioned. The officer threatened to take me to jail; even after the manager of the theater was satisfied I'd done no wrong. I explained that I'd walked in and out of two other screening rooms during the fifteen to twenty minutes I had before my movie began. The manager agreed to my offer to pay for two more movies to appease the cop.

When I tried to explain to him I was an honest man and a father, and had not done what he was accusing me of, he said, "Shut up, homeboy. I should take your ass to jail." I continued to respectfully listen while he berated me like I was a child who got caught with his hand in the cookie jar.

At home stewing over the humiliating encounter, I decided to take the diplomatic approach to reconcile the issue. I went back to the theater and calmly and diplomatically, addressed the officer about the temperament he'd displayed during our prior encounter and expressed the intent to report him. The gentler approach sparked a conversation lasting two to three hours, where we discussed several subjects including Martin Luther King Jr., Malcolm X, and civil rights. Through the discussion, we discovered we were both family men doing our best to navigate around the pitfalls of life and working to provide the best for our family. It was a genuinely fun and informative conversation and we parted with a handshake.

I happened to see the officer a few days later as I pulled beside him at a stoplight. "Mr. Singleton, how are you?" he asked through his window. "I'm fine, sir. How are you? Good to see you." I pulled away, pondering the power of diplomatic communication. I credit that moment with the inspiration to write, produce, direct, and star in my first movie, *White Man, Black Man, Jew Man*—a film emphasizing the importance of communication in order to solve the ills of our society.

These experiences proved good things could come from bad situations as long as we're willing to take a calm, reasonable, and open approach to solving them.

But good things still weren't happening fast enough for me in Los Angeles. There were no open doors for me in Hollywood. Not even doors with anyone on the other side willing to turn the lock and help me through. My time in L.A. was over.

I'd arrived with no real contacts or knowledge about the way Hollywood works and would leave with a host of knowledge to carry me forward. I had a wife and children at home who needed me. Family responsibilities were top priority. The right priority, I told myself as I packed the car for the ride home.

The drive back was one long thinking process. Part of the time I was miserable, embarrassed I had achieved nothing, angry I'd gone all the way across the country on a mission I viewed as a failure. As the road stretched on and on, I felt like I would never get back to Atlanta. Never reach my destination. I feared I'd spend days driving down roads without end, trapped in some horrific alternate dimension of personal suffering where all I did was spin my wheels. I shed tears more than once as the City of Angels faded from view behind me.

By the time I'd entered Texas, my thought process began to shift toward a more productive focus. Whatever I wanted to do at this juncture in my life, it needed to be done in Atlanta—that much was clear from my experience. I would go back to L.A. in the future with a more robust résumé, I promised myself, and work to develop contacts that could aid me in getting the kind of meetings I needed to achieve the success I sought. It didn't matter how long it'd take. Heck, it didn't even matter if I physically made it back to Los Angeles. Plenty of people had robust, fulfilling careers of note in locations outside Tinseltown. I needed to think broader, bigger than I had been.

"Look at how far you've traveled already," I said to the night air somewhere in Louisiana. Even though it wasn't going exactly according to the vision in my head, I was living my dream. I'd come out of the projects running full speed with the help of God and a growing understanding of what it meant to live a "good" life. And I wasn't just doing it for me; I was doing it for all of us. For anyone who strove for the light. I grew during my time in L.A., and added valuable lessons to my personal script I would carry forward and share with others.

In a way I was on a personal walkabout. I might not be traversing the Australian outback, but I was on a journey to transform myself. I thought I knew the destination of my quest, but accepted I may not have when I arrived in L.A. Even though there had been disappointments, and I would probably suffer more, I was on the right track.

I didn't stop often on my way back across the country. There wasn't much money for things like motels, and I was eager to get back to Atlanta. But crossing through Louisiana, my appetite returned and I decided to hit a fast food joint on one of my pit stops to fill the Mazda's tank. Chicken and biscuits, with sweet tea to wash it all down. I smiled as I nibbled on the chicken's crispy coating. It tasted like home.

Chapter 26
Bitter Pills

I laughed behind my mask as my mother-in-law Barbara hopped around the birthday party, tickling and joking with all the toddler boys who'd joined us for E.Z.'s celebration. She was dressed up in a bunny costume for our son Ethereal Zephyr's special day. Commaleta, as usual, was behind the camera snapping pictures of the partygoers, catching moments that might seem trivial, but we would cherish the memories later. She was a photographer; with a keen eye for the way light surrounds an individual or object.

I wasn't quite sure whether I was imagining it, but it looked like Commaleta was angling to sneak around behind her mother. When she reached her destination and pointed the video camera towards her mother's fluffy tail, I was hit with a full-fledged giggle fit. I wondered if my mother-in-law realized how silly she looked. Then I remembered I was wearing tight black pants, a sleeved shirt with vertically aligned diamonds on each arm, a gaudy yellow belt, and a full head-covering face mask. I was a Power Ranger. I giggled even harder.

E.Z. was probably a few years too young to understand my costume. When I'd emerged from the back of our home in Summer Glen, he and the other boys cringed in fear and backed away. But once I revealed my Power Ranger persona, I had to follow through or risk creating a lifelong fear of the character. I ran forward, tripping on purpose over my feet and tumbling to the ground. I got up and lumbered toward them, threatening a tickle attack, only to "trip" again and land on my backside. The boys started to giggle. One of the young boys gathered up the gumption to launch a counter-attack. Once he came charging toward me, the others followed suit and it was a free-for-all melee taking us across the backyard, over and under the trampoline and all the way to the back porch where the other parents waited with the cake.

It was November 2010. Our youngest had just turned seven and after years of what could only generously be called modest progress, my career outlook was pretty favorable. I watched my son and his friends dive into the birthday treats and couldn't stop smiling.

* * * * * * * * *

As the long months turned into years after my return from Los Angeles, the only acting projects coming my way were small, "no budget" gigs. I wrote comedy routines, raps, and screenplays in every spare minute I had between a series of odd jobs making just enough to provide food for our table when added to Commaleta's income from the Professional Standards Commission. The series of jobs included mascot work for Mascots of America, the Atlanta Braves baseball team, and other professional sports organizations throughout Atlanta; refereeing basketball, softball and football for local sporting events; working part-time hours at the Westin Peachtree Hotel as a server; and emceeing events. I even spent a year loading luggage on and off of planes at the Atlanta airport. None of those jobs were even remotely close to what I wanted to do. We decided to make the stagnation count toward something worth a sacrifice so I put my acting career on the backburner, contacted my old friend Greg at Subway in Buckhead and went back to work there as a store manager, giving Commaleta the opportunity to pursue her Master's Degree in Information Technology while still working for the state of Georgia.

In an effort to combine my theatrical talent with the reality that we needed to forge our own way, Commaleta and I decided to open up a small costume store. Family members helped us run the store, so we could keep our other jobs and own a business. I planned to augment our income by doing costumed appearances at birthday parties and other events. It wasn't my dream situation, but it would keep me in the game until the next big project came along.

To open the shop, we had to leverage ourselves to the hilt. No bank was willing to give us a loan, so Commaleta and I maxed out our credit cards and took out a second mortgage to get it off the ground. We taught ourselves how to create a business plan, file taxes, and shopped around for suppliers and a good location.

Our costume store, Pardi Gras'tumes, opened in August 2003—three months before our third child was due. Our main focus understandably, was Halloween costumes from infant through adult plus-sizes. We wanted the store to be family oriented. A place we could bring our own children, so we didn't stock a large quantity of super grotesque costumes. A few ghouls, goblins, and ghosts haunted the shop, but most of our shelves were lined with princesses and super heroes, animal and sports-themed costumes. For appearances at events, we stocked up on some pop-culture favorite costumes I could wear. Batman. Spiderman. The Incredible Hulk. Darth Vader. A Power Ranger. We did very well right out of the gate, posting strong sales moving into the Halloween period.

We'd also run into a period of high stress in our personal life when we were trying to get the business off the ground. I'd like to say it was merely work-related stress, but the truth was, it was me. I'd been keeping a secret from Commaleta for a couple of years. It concerned actions I had prayed for God's forgiveness for several times, but had yet to confide in my wife. It weighed heavily on my conscience. A few weeks before Ethereal was born, I confessed.

I waited until we were lying in bed to lay my burden out for her. When I started, Commaleta was already groggy and halfway asleep. But by the time I finished saying, "I don't even know how to tell you this, I don't want to hurt you, but I *have* to," she was wide-awake.

During my time touring with *Sugar Daddy* back in 2000, when Commaleta was pregnant with Nevvaeh, I'd had several opportunities to mix and mingle with women across the country. There was rarely any interaction beyond the normal sort of social pleasantries one exchanges at a cocktail reception or a blues lounge. But on two occasions, temptation and the ghosts of my past set me on a path of lust and deceit. March 18, 2000, three months after I had said my marriage vows, was the date I fully invalidated my claim to manhood.

Another *Sugar Daddy* cast mate had a lady friend who traveled from Jacksonville to Orlando to hook up with him after seeing our show. She brought a friend along and wondered if my cast mate had someone who could accompany her for the evening. I acquiesced and went with him to their hotel room for an evening of drinking and laughing. It degenerated quickly into a decadent, lustful, landfill of debauchery. With my cast mate and his lady friend on one bed soaking the sheets, the immoral familiarity of sexual domination I'd accommodated in the past regained control of my mind, and I found myself following suit. I laid with the woman for all of four or five strokes.

Shame and disgust I thought I'd buried alive and concealed in the innermost tomb of my core rejuvenated and became exponentially more powerful with each successive stroke. The reality of what I was doing exploded in my head in the form of a great ball of terror and sparked a damning inner soliloquy that would have impressed the most avid of Shakespeare enthusiasts.

I jumped out of the bed and ran to the sink practically screaming, "What the fuck have I done?"

I scrubbed my penis like a dishwasher scrubbing a scorched pan that'd held a burnt porterhouse steak. *What is wrong with me?* I berated myself and stole a quick, tentative glance at the fool in the mirror.

The rough part of my life was over. God had spared me from a life of misery and made way for an abundant life of bliss. I was at a point where I had total control over my actions and fully understood the ramifications. God had given me a queen and she accepted all my shortcomings. Commaleta stuck by my side through my acne-riddled teenage years when society had written me off like a bad check. She supported me when the naysayers said someone from my circumstances wasn't worth the time. She was there for me when our high school history teacher, Ms. Singletary, told her she was too good for me. She even disregarded her mother's advice to avoid a project boy with no future, and her aunt's intensely colorful admonitions to stay away from "pissy" young project thugs. The only thing that mattered to her was the potential she saw in me others did not—something special enough to gamble her entire future on.

My morals had been trampled by sin. I continued my aggressive, but futile attempt to scrub away more than the woman's essence drying on me, but the guilt ate me alive from the inside out. When I looked in the mirror, I did not like myself. I was disgusted with whom I saw. God was not proud of me. Like Adam and Eve in the Garden of Eden, my fig leaf had been removed. My shame erupted and spewed like lava from a volcano. I had been defeated.

Instead of stopping me in my tracks, the incident provided a gateway to another risqué encounter. The second woman was a cast mate who persisted in coming to my room to flirt whenever my roommate was gone. Eventually, she ended up with her pants down with my fingers exploring her inner walls. I didn't see much harm in doing it; I had already committed the ultimate sin.

But something was different with her. I had no desire to have sex like in the past. I had transcended beyond the need to demonstrate my sexual power. As I proceeded to play with her, it became clear I had no intention of consummating the debauchery. There was nothing more than the immoral familiarity piquing my curiosity and provoking a moment of indulgence. It was the thrill of a chase gone too far.

I was happy and relieved I didn't go all the way. I was dead set on re-validating my honor and restoring my commitment of fidelity to Commaleta. In a weird and distorted way, I felt a small sense of victory in knowing I had control over my penis. Although I didn't have sex with the second woman, I had still broken my promise to my wife. Again.

* * * * * * * * *

Commaleta darn near lost her mind when I told her. Through omission and deception, beyond the heinous breach of our commitment to each other and to our family, I had kept the information from her for over two years.

"After everything we've been through … this? Now? How could you do this to me, to us … to our children? I thought we had moved beyond this, Robert. I trusted you with every ounce of my being, with my life. God! How could you allow this? After everything I've committed to you. I've given you all of me and this is my reward?"

After asking me why I had chosen this moment to come clean, when we were launching a business and expecting a child, she pulled back. Commaleta told me the timing of my confession was selfish and hurtful beyond any excuse known to man. She whipped through the bedroom like a storm, sweeping knickknacks off our dresser and ripping clothing out of the closet. Then she spent over an hour in the bathroom, crying behind the locked door.

Commaleta raged over the betrayal, demanding to know how this could have happened. "You told me this was where I needed to be," she shouted. She yanked the bathroom closet open, where the shelves were lined in perfect arrangement. Attacking, she tossed items on the floor.

At first I thought she was talking to me, but as she continued to stomp around the bathroom, I realized the horrible truth. Her faith had been shaken by my actions.

"I trusted you, your guidance. I put my faith in Rob. And after everything, after all the trials and tribulations, the forgiveness, the battle for trust, this is what I get? You have betrayed me." Her voice started to shake. She emerged from the bathroom and backed up against the bedroom wall when she caught sight of me. She clutched a pair of dress slacks and slid down the wall. "God, how could you?"

Through my tears, I stared at Commaleta from the bed and wondered what, if anything, I could do to reach out to her. There had to be some way to support her through her anguish, to make up for the damage I'd done. But I knew there was nothing to do.

My actions had rattled her to the core, and had left her questioning the one constant in all our lives. To rob someone of their faith, even temporarily, was one of the worst sins I could have committed. I had caused a lot of pain. The same pain I had experienced in former years. I saw people shot and one killed in the past, but never in my life could I fathom the amount of pain I could inflict upon this beautiful flower who shared my bed, my life.

It was demented, like I wouldn't find satisfaction until I had administered enough pain to match what I had experienced in my own life. And I had done it to the one individual on earth whom I loved most and who was least deserving of it. If she had murdered me in my sleep, it would not have been morally justified, but I would have understood.

I unfolded my legs from under me and slid to the side of the bed. Without a word, I rose and walked out of the room. The sounds of her sobs followed me down the hall.

* * * * * * * * *

Over the course of the next several weeks, I struggled to diffuse her anger. The day after my revelation, it became painfully obvious Commaleta was on the verge of walking out for good. Yes, she had two kids to care for and a third on the way and didn't know what she would do, but she realized her loss of faith should be directed at only one target—me. Somehow I convinced her to sit down long enough to let me try to explain. I brought our girls downstairs and sat them on the couch.

They regarded me with fear and confusion in their eyes. I dropped down to my knees in front of them. "Daddy messed up, girls. I messed up good. I've betrayed you all. You, your mom. I've hurt you all in a way I never would have expected." Tears welled up in my eyes and spilled down my cheeks. I vowed to them this would never happen again. I would prove myself worthy of their forgiveness and if they gave me another chance, I would not let them down. "I don't know if your mother can ever forgive me, but as God is my witness, I will never make this mistake again. Never."

Even as I stated my case, I wondered how many other men out there made similar pronouncements after being unfaithful. I guessed there weren't many who confessed of their own accord without getting caught in the act. I didn't know about the legitimacy of other unfaithful men, but I knew how I felt. Waves of nausea rolled through me, so strong I thought every organ in my belly was going to fly out. My mouth was dry and I didn't have enough liquid left in my body after all the crying to produce spit to swallow. "I *will* make this right," I promised them.

Commaleta was furious. I'd backed her into a corner where she was not only battling her own emotions, but those of our kids. The girls heard my plea and pestered Commaleta, arguing since I had admitted my crimes, I should be given a second chance. She didn't have the heart to tell them I'd already had my second chance … and a third. She viewed my approach warily, suspicious I'd purposely gone to our children in order to force her to stay. It wasn't a strategy I'd planned on, but I couldn't deny I would do anything, anything at all, to keep our family together. The only thing I knew for certain was I had to keep them around long enough to prove from the very depths of my soul I was truly contrite.

To say Commaleta was still angry with me the day she went into labor would be a gross understatement. She'd agreed to stay, to try and continue moving forward. But there was a significant trust deficit in the Singleton household. We trooped to the hospital to welcome our son, Ethereal, early on a Saturday morning. Commaleta's mother came with us, taking up a position next to her daughter's bedside as she'd done for the births of Heavven and Nevvaeh.

But the costume shop needed to be open and running. It was the week after Halloween—a strong sales period for costume retailers as consumers sought out post-holiday deals. We could not afford to be closed. I made her leave—over her objections and those of my labor-weary wife—to go take care of the store. Commaleta glared at me after her mother left. But it wasn't the endearing, "I'm in labor you son of a bitch, this is all your fault," look many women get while in the throes of labor.

For the rest of the year we were not so much a married couple and more a couple inmates crammed into a prison cell and forced to survive together. Commaleta was never overtly cruel; it was not in her nature. She was distant and largely unconcerned with anything I was going through or attempting to do with work. I could barely get her to sit down and look over the new play I was writing. I wanted Commaleta to see it because I viewed the play as part of owning up to what I'd done, part of my penance. But at least she was still there. I could walk around the house and throw my arms around my children at will. I prayed for God to give me the time to earn her forgiveness, to prove I was finally man enough to be a part of the family. Though my interactions with my wife remained stilted and painful, I dared to hope we would make it through.

Commaleta's mother continued to work the shop weekdays, with one of us or Commaleta's brother and sister coming in to help on the weekends. It was a difficult period. Beyond our personal difficulties, the shop had failed to do well after our opening and Halloween. The money we were paying my mother-in-law for her work came out of the paychecks from our other jobs. We weren't making enough money at the costume shop on a regular basis to have enough funds to cover rent, bills, supplies, or even a meager salary for our sole employee. We were juggling work schedules—with mine occasionally taking me out of town to emcee an event—raising three kids, running a household, managing our business, and trying to make forward progress financially.

Toward the end of our shop's first year, the cornerstone retail outlet in the small plaza where our store was located—a grocery store—closed down as a result of a lackluster economy. It cost the area a lot of retail traffic, and hit us hard. The only event I'd done a costumed appearance for was a friend's child's birthday at a deeply discounted fee. We had yet to generate enough business to recover more than a small percentage of our initial investment and our hopes of any improvements were dimming.

We'd learned our lessons over the last year. When the Halloween sale season ended, our costume shop would be no more.

Chapter 27
The Resurrected

I didn't care if the audience laughed at me or booed me off the stage. This was it. Just me and the lights, laying bare the truths of all the lessons I'd learned to anyone who cared to see it. I would hold nothing back on the stage. I stood backstage at the 14th Street Playhouse in Midtown Atlanta and waited for the music cueing me to step out in front of the audience.

The mirror behind the stage in the dressing area reflected a man dressed in a black tank top, jeans, and belt. There was no fancy makeup or elaborate costuming, here. It was just IronE—a boy who'd come out of the projects, crippled by the environment and the mentality of failure, to be reborn through experience into a man determined to live a successful, good life. I wasn't worried about being judged for what I'd done. God was my judge and jury. All the challenges I'd faced, the mistakes I'd made, were worth nothing if I couldn't use my experience to share with others. Not from a place of self-righteousness, but understanding the desperation, the lure of a fast life. And the debilitating emotional costs accompanying the struggle to find a way out.

I had been working on the play—*IronE: the Resurrected*—for a long time before it debuted in August 2008. Not the writing. The words came quickly once I'd realized they were right in front of me. For years I'd bumbled and fumbled, thinking I knew the way—that the destination was the reward.

Only recently had I understood what God had been trying to tell me for so long. The journey itself was an integral part of the purpose. Everything I'd done, each decision I'd made, was a part of the story … something I could relay to others in the hopes of helping them make different mistakes than I had.

The costume shop, and a few other minor and less successful

business endeavors, decimated our finances, left us with unpaid bills, and sporadic service cut-offs in an ongoing cat-n-mouse game with bill collectors. We had no viable options to fund *IronE: The Resurrected* other than pawning our car. We didn't get a lot, but it was enough to rent space at the 14th Street Playhouse's Stage 3. Two high school friends, Free and Chebria Wastson, gave us two hundred dollars to cover necessities and give us a little breathing room during the pre-run prep.

Commaleta ran the show as stage manager and also handled sound. My theater buddy from UGA, Jazz, introduced the production and then ran the video. Big Larry ushered the audience to their seats, serving as house manager. My sister-in-law, Carlesha—Ke—was the photographer and babysat the kids while they read, played, and watched movies backstage in my dressing room. It seemed like only yesterday Commaleta and I were babysitting Ke and my brother-in-law Makiyal—Ki.

With thirteen years on them, Commaleta and I took the role of parental figures, hoping our guidance and dedication would help them avoid many of the mistakes we'd made during our journey. There were many years we would load up our vehicles with Ke, Ki, my nephews Edward—Ed—and Tyreecio—Reeci—and many other kids in the family and head south to Daytona, Florida to expose them to things they otherwise wouldn't experience because of their circumstances.

Sadly, despite our efforts and strong involvement, many of the young men we embraced chose roads in life like my brother Tracy. Their path forced them to face life's lessons from a more rigid perspective, leaving an impression on their character society would hold against them for the remainder of their lives. Watching the lives of many of our loved ones spiral downward, despite positive guidance, helped ignite the flames of desperation and fuel the passion to give birth to *Resurrected*. I had to share my story with the world in hopes of saving lives on a larger scale.

For months in advance, Commaleta and I rehearsed the play in our garage late at night after we put the kids to bed—working on my timing, preparing to reveal to the world at large things I'd only told those closest to me. Commaleta had stuck by me and somehow managed to find it within her heart to help me do this after everything I'd put her through. She truly believed in what I was trying to accomplish and helped counter any nervous energy I suffered as we worked to make my dream a tangible reality.

* * * * * * * * *

I stepped out on to the bare stage. My only props for the show were a folding chair and a four by four foot-high platform. I was ready. Failure found me so many times before, I was no longer afraid. My formal and informal training prepared me for this moment. Behind me hung a banner for the show, the title surrounded by images of an eagle, flames, and the comedy-tragedy masks synonymous not only with the theater, but iconic images spawning philosophical examinations of the dual nature of man for eons. The rest of the stage's backdrop was a plain black curtain—a looming shadow behind the bright lights.

I began each performance on my knees, my head bent in prayer, before rising from the ground for the opening monologue.

"I feel my life has gone from the abyss to the utopia-end of the spiritual spectrum. I've come from an environment where I was spiritually dead, my conscience for the most part … dormant. My way of thinking, speaking, acting, was an act of socialization …

"Through God's grace and guidance, I have and will continue to do great things with my life, until, the day I die."

It was a promise I made to myself, to my family and one I now made to the audience with the full expectation they hold me to it. As the words escaped my mouth, the crashing of breaking glass shattered my reverie. It was the sound of a young child, raging in a bathroom with his face covered in cake and ice cream. The opening scene in a decade of violence—guns, drugs, sex, and the death of a drug-addicted mother afflicted by HIV/AIDS—helping to build the foundation from which I would grow.

"The aforementioned is not just the synopsis for a stage play, but it is my life story," I continued, hoping the audience would agree to come on this journey with me, even if for a little while.

"Although most would contend it would be better if the gloomy part had only been the plot to a stage play, I respectfully disagree. The adage I use is—what would triumph be without tragedy? That's the dualistic structure of nature. To paraphrase the famous philosopher Rene Descartes, how would one recognize good without bad, peace without war? I am the sum of all my life experiences.

"I am an eagle in flight, with a spirit unbroken … dedication to my maker and an homage to homies. I introduced 'em to the drug game. They fell short. It's a shame. But your memories live on in the E Hall of Fame. For the record, y'all some soldiers serving life in the 'hood. Tell Martin Luther and the rest magnifique, they did good. Laying it down on the line, that's what true soldiers do. No matter what, at all costs, you sacrifice for your crew," I continued, raising my head and hand up to God.

"But I'll holla, I'll be coming through," I told God and everyone who had gone on to the afterlife before me. "But not before I handle the business, and do what I came here to do."

As the final words left my lips, the stage went dark … and the resurrection began.

The play jumped ahead to the twenty-second century. An Indian professor—with an Asian and a Hispanic student asking questions—discussed black American history, the human condition, and the effects of music, entertainment, and technology on the moral fabric of the country. How black American penchant for loud music, dance, and drinking in the closing and early decades of the twentieth and twenty-first centuries, respectively, led to their extinction.

"To understand this group's downfall, we must understand that their ignorance led to their extinction," the Indian professor said to the audience. "Can you imagine? Such a people who would destroy themselves? And I know, I know, some of you are asking 'what about the educated African Americans?' Well they got a skin-whitening procedure, what we refer to as the 'Off the Wall' makeover, and blended in with the rest of society."

I had practiced for months to get not only the accent, but also the common mannerisms of a believable Indian persona, to a point where it looked legit. And it was fun. While the scene depicted some heavy thoughts about the bleak future I saw, not just for African American life and culture, but for all humanity, if we did not collectively work to change the direction, I wanted the professor to make the audience feel comfortable with the learning process as I continued to perform.

"In my appreciation for life, liberty, and the pursuit of

happiness, I realized that the rights secured for all through the constitution, not only excluded women—that's obvious in its reference that 'all men are created equal'—but it excluded any other group that wasn't white. More particularly, black people because blacks weren't considered human at that time. Therefore, slavery and the brutal mistreatment of blacks were justified. In my quest for truth and knowledge, the question of why haunted me until I was forced to beg the question: Why does suffering seem to have affected not just my mother or my family lineage or black people, but all people—the whole of humanity?

"God then revealed to me that we, as human beings, subject ourselves to the suffering we endure because we fail to acknowledge our oneness with each other. We let our conquest for worldly passions and riches dominate and suppress our spiritual essence. And unfortunately, race, religion, and politics are sometimes distorted and used as veils of deceit to camouflage this intent—hence, war, and destruction. To deny this assertion is to deny your existence as an intelligent being spawned from the all-inclusive supreme source. This war to which I'm referring is a lot more dangerous than America's Civil War or World Wars I & II, Vietnam, Iraq, and even a Nuclear War. It is the war goin' on inside each and every one of us. The conscience. Do we choose to do right or do we choose to do wrong?

"Gandhi said it best when he said, 'the worst wars are fought in the heart of man.' Yes! There is a war goin' on inside of us each and every conscious minute of our lives. I am determined righteousness will prevail as the victor in me. What about you?"

We used music to switch between snapshots of my formative years, with my self-penned raps filling in some of the blanks for the audience. Street fights. Pregnant crack addicts. Drug deals. Lil' Larry hiding in the bedroom closet. Lost, troubled souls looking for love and understanding in a world where the strong preyed on the weak, where the need for income blanketed dreams of a better future in a suffocating mass of bad decisions and dwindling options. A place where truth and love were often little more than chalk lines on a criminal-infested street corner, left to be washed away by the rain.

"It's my duty to do what I do ... to make sure this doesn't happen to you," I told the audience.

But my story would be incomplete without the light shining through the darkness. My faith in God. Commaleta. Football. Accomplishment through hard work. My children. Family. For each of us, there are people, situations, and places put in our paths to help us battle whatever darkness creeps into our lives. For so many of us, it is easier to ignore the extension of hope from rays of truth and love—and the work that is required to hold on to them—and embrace the easier options before us, like so many of the people I grew up with.

* * * * * * * * *

When the time came for the 14th Street Playhouse staff to take *IronE: the Resurrected* down from the marquee, only a few dozen people had seen the play during the five-day run at the theater. I hoped those who saw me lay my soul bare would remember the experience and take it with them as a testimony. In some way, I wanted my efforts to touch them and help them go forth with truth and love in their hearts. Of course I wanted the play to go on an endless run to sellout crowds every night, but I also understood part of the resurrection concept was new beginnings. I hadn't realized, sitting in the crowd—visible as silhouettes behind the stage lights shining in my eyes—was an Atlanta-based theatrical agent. Someone with their eye out for local actors who could fill roles in the film and television boom heading Atlanta's way.

Chapter 28
Blindsided

He was me. At least he should have been, statistically speaking—a moneygrubbing full-fledged thug with no care for anyone else but himself. I knew as soon as I saw the sides—the audition piece—for Alton, this was the role I was born to play. It wasn't just life in Hurt Village being portrayed in the film; it *was* life in Perry Homes. I knew Alton well from a few lines of dialogue—like he was my brother— and it terrified me. My fear drove me to deliver the best audition of my life.

I was so confident in the performance; I told Commaleta and Big Larry, "This is my role." I honestly believed there was no trained actor out there who could live the character the way I could. God ordained the role, and He allowed me to survive through everything I had gone through for this particular moment in my life. For two weeks, every time the phone rang I was convinced it was my agent from Houghton Talent with good news. I would be acting beside Sandra Bullock in a major feature film. By the time the third week rolled around, there was no doubt I had somehow missed the mark. My Alton, as real as he may have been in my mind, may not have been the performance they were looking for.

I tried my best to put it out of my mind. When the caller ID on the phone said Houghton Talent a few weeks later, I didn't figure *The Blind Side* would be the reason for the call. In April 2009, I strolled on to the set of *The Blind Side* and it was like walking back through time.

Shooting scenes for *The Blind Side* in a closed-down Atlanta housing project—Thomasville Heights—opposite Sandra Bullock and Quinton Aaron had a surreal dreamy quality to it. Production crewmembers moved carefully around the cameras, lights, microphones and various cables accompanying them, as we prepared to film. Meanwhile, the extras cast as street thugs were in costume and in character, sauntering around joking, and roughhousing with one another. Everyone on set was professional, but it was easy to get lost in the moment at home on the Atlanta streets. It was an odd mix of two worlds; they didn't seem to go together, but made perfect sense to me.

The Blind Side was based on the real-life story of Michael Oher. Like me, he was born into poverty, but found a way to overcome. With help from his adopted family, the Tuohy's, Oher performed well in high school and was recruited to play college ball at the University of Mississippi before going on to a successful career as an offensive lineman in the National Football League.

My first major scene had Alton sitting on a stoop, asserting his street cred front of a group of young men when Mrs. Tuohy visits Michael's 'hood Hurt Village for the first time. Big Mike forced Mrs. Tuohy to stay in the car while he went to look for his mother, and my character Alton took the opportunity to taunt her from afar. The scene contained what was probably my favorite line, "Hey D, watch this … they always go for the wink. Bim."

Later in the film, when Big Mike went back to the projects looking for his mother, Alton let him know it was just about her normal time to stop in and grab a rock to smoke, and invites him in for a "forty." Alton offers Mike a spot on *his* team of project businessmen. But when Alton jokes with Michael about sleeping with Mrs. Tuohy or her daughter, it triggers an outright brawl.

Alton's final scene with Bullock's Tuohy became one of the most popular moments in the Academy Award-nominated film. In fact, it was one of the scenes selected for broadcast during the 2010 Oscars, where Bullock won the best actress award. Touhy headed to the 'hood looking for Michael and encounters a beat up, pissed off Alton instead. The two have a verbal altercation where they call each other bitch. I threw everything I had at her in every take we filmed.

"Whatchu got in there? .22? A little Saturday night special?" Alton taunted.

"Mm-hmm. And it shoots just fine every other day of the week, too."

While my character Alton exhibited nothing but disdain for

Touhy's efforts to help Michael Oher leave the want of childhood behind for success as an adult, I couldn't have felt more different about the actor portraying this kindhearted woman. She was classy and kind.

I hung around the set after we'd finished shooting for the day, talking to some of the local extras on the project when I felt a tap on my right shoulder. I turned around and found myself face-to-face with America's favorite "girl next door." She threw her arms around me and gave me a big hug, commending me for my performance, saying I had genuinely wowed her and creeped her out at the same time. Sandy told me she panicked a little when she saw what I was putting out there, wondering how she'd be able to respond in kind. She looked forward to seeing me in Hollywood and hoped we would have the chance to work together again in the future. I'd like to say I mustered a snappy debonair response, but truthfully I was a little dumbstruck by her generosity. This actress—who already had an amazing body of work behind her, who was a genuine Hollywood A-lister, and was under no obligation to come over and talk to me at all—had validated my efforts. I was so stunned and grateful; I felt the sting of tears at the back of my eyes.

Watching her walk away, I let her words wash over me, and felt like I had finally made it. In a strange way the circle was complete. I had worked hard to get out of the 'hood and there was so much more work ahead of me. But here I was participating in a project paralleling my experiences; a project I hoped would inspire young boys and girls to reach for something better, the way Oher had. I knew a movie with director John Lee Hancock and outstanding cast would turn out well. The film, a massive critical and commercial success, was a testament not only to the hard work everyone put in on the project, but the power of the message as well. When someone is in need, regardless of who they are or where they're from, you help them if you can. It is the meaning of truth and love.

The film came into my life at the opportune moment. Years of little professional progress left me questioning how best to have a real impact, to spread the message of truth and love to a wider audience. I'd considered a lot of possibilities, including a return to school to pursue a law degree and taking a stab at politics. The choices were limitless. The sky the only limit. If I played my cards right, I could even be the first black American president. But then a one-time Senator from Illinois named Barack Obama stormed onto the national political stage in a meteoric rise to the Oval Office. The night of Obama's election, I was elated the United States had elected a black president, and sad it was a first I'd never achieve.

Commaleta still laughs when she remembers my reaction on the historic night. After the final numbers came in and Obama was declared the winner, I headed downstairs to join my wife. I descended slowly down the stairs, tears blurring my vision. "Well, I guess that wasn't God's plan for me," I told her. Commaleta looked at me kindly, a smile tugging at the sides of her mouth.

Even with the uncertainty I faced, I knew if I kept searching for ways to move forward, God's plan for me would be revealed. Within a few months, I stood on set with Bullock crafting a message we hoped millions would receive.

The Blind Side ends with Oher being selected by the Baltimore Ravens as a first round draft pick, a man with a bright future ahead of him. A future that would take him and the Ravens to a Super Bowl victory in the 2012-2013 season. When I saw the finished product at the New York premiere, I understood immediately the impact this work would have—and I was ready for more.

Chapter 29
Meeting the Dead

The Atlanta weather was not cooperating. Oh, it was doing what it normally would any summer, but it was so blisteringly hot, sweat evaporated off our skin into the atmosphere as fast as our bodies could produce it. It felt like the sun would never set. Being an Atlanta native gave me an advantage over my colleagues, but not much. Hot is hot, used to it or not. And we were all searching for shade and liquids any chance we got.

I spent most of the day lying on my back after getting my face punched in. And to be honest, I was kind of grateful. Down on the ground it seemed to be marginally cooler. The shadows of the folks still standing loomed over me, and being on the ground meant I had to exert less energy for a few minutes. My peers—Laurie Holden, Steven Yeun, Juan Pareja, Jeryl Prescott Sales, and the others around them—staggered under the heat, leaned on walls, downed bottles of water, and tried their best not to show their pain or complain on the roof of the Norfolk Southern building.

The man who kept straddling me to sit on my chest had different ideas. He wasn't going to let me off the hook. I expected no less from an individual like Michael Rooker. I looked down at my chest in horror as he spat on my shirt and rubbed it in … not for the first time that day.

The first major character conflict in AMC's new television show, *The Walking Dead*, unfolded on this downtown Atlanta rooftop.

We'd taken some time before we began shooting to discuss the scene and how we wanted to handle the fighting involved. According to the script, Michael's character—a doped-up redneck named Merle Dixon—was supposed to toss racial epithets at my

169

character, T-Dog, before getting the better of him in a fistfight. I was a little awestruck watching this living legend run through the blows he wanted to throw, how he would aim at the various parts of my face. As Michael spoke, I had no doubt he would never miss a mark. He joked and smiled, talking through the scene's action, but there was a piercing gleam in his blue eyes to let me know he was deadly serious. From the precise way he moved it was clear this wasn't a man you'd want to mess with if the fight wasn't scripted.

This was it, right here. This was the reason I ended up on a zombie show, sitting in a stuffy stairwell—watching an actor whose work I'd long admired prepare to kick my butt—on a show with another legend at the helm; Frank Darabont.

* * * * * * * * *

When my agent first came to me with the audition for *The Walking Dead* I wasn't sure I'd get the role, or even want it. A horror television show with violence, blood, and guts? I'd spent my life battling against violence, against any loss of life from drugs, guns, alcohol, or any other cause barring accidents or natural death. I wasn't really a horror fan in general. Freddie, Jason, Michael ... those guys freaked me out well into adulthood. From as early as I could remember, my mother would take me and Tracy to see almost every horror movie in the theaters to see who was courageous enough to watch without covering their eyes. I was the more courageous one. Not only did my brother cover his eyes most times, he often fell asleep to avoid the monsters up on the screen. Maybe I should have followed suit because I'd been traumatized ever since.

Needless to say, this show didn't sound like it was really my thing. But when I heard Darabont and Gale Anne Hurd were attached to it, there was no doubt I wanted to give it a shot and I took a closer look at the sides. From the information I had to base my audition on, T-Dog was someone who had a less revolting personality than Alton from *The Blind Side*, but was definitely still a guy from the street. A call from Darabont's office let my agent know they'd appreciated my attempt at the rooftop dialogue, but he wanted to see me play the character straighter, less 'hood. After my second audition went through, I was offered the role of T-Dog in AMC's new show for two, maybe three, episodes.

I didn't know much more about *The Walking Dead* than what Commaleta or I could find from a basic Internet search. The show was based off a popular comic book I'd never heard of, created by a man named Robert Kirkman—who played a big part in the development of his story for television. In it a group of survivors from around the Atlanta area battle hordes of zombies after an infection wipes out most of the U.S. population. Any reservations I had about the messages the show would send or the behavior it could encourage disappeared after our first cast meeting a couple days before I began shooting.

I walked into a room filled with a disparate group of people, most of whom I had checked out online beforehand and was excited to work with. There was a man with dark hair and Mediterranean skin coloring. His build screamed "trained athlete." I noted his well-formed arm muscles when he reached out to shake my hand and told me his name was Jon Bernthal. Standing nearby was a slender brunette whose captivating smile was set to "stun mode." I recognized Sarah Wayne Callies from her time on *Prison Break*. I moved around the room greeting the others—a friendly Darabont production veteran named Laurie Holden, former Atlanta commercial casting director Melissa McBride who had once auditioned me for a commercial, a young boy—no older than nine or ten—named Chandler Riggs and Michael Rooker. If the face I'd seen so many times on the screen didn't spark an immediate recognition, Rooker's unique gravelly voice would have done it the moment he opened his mouth. Two men entered the room behind me—a tall, lanky gentleman with a crisp British accent who introduced himself as Andrew Lincoln, and visionary director Frank Darabont.

Darabont's energy filled the room. He walked up to each individual and shook their hand, expressing his excitement to each actor in turn about their participation in the project. He made us feel welcome before inviting everyone to take a seat to do a round of quick introductions before the group began reading.

In a windowless room in the production offices on Elsworth—near the corner of Huff Street—the scripts laid in front of us on the oval table were brilliant. Darabont and crew had created an atmospheric piece of art where the monsters viewers expected weren't always the monsters in reality. We would be bashing in plenty of zombie brains, but it was the human drama, human frailty, and the drive to survive steering the show right from the get-go. As the read-through progressed, I realized I had been mistaken. It wasn't a horror project; it was an examination of humanity. Darabont wanted the apocalypse to be as real to us as possible, to be an organic extension of who we were as people. And as we read through the lines of episode two, I was glad to be a part of it.

* * * * * * * * *

The production crew grappled with setting up the safety mat and cameras at the precise angles needed to get the shot of T-Dog being driven to the ground by Merle's onslaught. He would start the fight with a rifle butt to my face and lunge, punching me. On the ground, I'd take a couple kicks in the ribs, have a gun pointed in my face, and be spit on in a show of dominance.

After a long hard look at the man throwing the punches I told them to abandon the setup change. "Let's just get this shot," I proclaimed, confident I could take the falls without seriously injuring myself and didn't need the mat.

The moment the words came out of my mouth, I knew I was truly invested. As an actor it's part of your job to never just go through the motions. We have to strive to become one with the character. *But this was different somehow.* I surveyed the crowd of sweaty red-faced actors and crew on the rooftop. The scene we were filming laid bare the current of latent racism cutting through the underbelly of every society; of the fight for control individuals strive for in order to determine their own fate, without the message being preachy or slogan-laden. It was, as Frank urged, very real.

* * * * * * * * *

T-Dog survived in the land of *The Walking Dead* longer than I'd originally anticipated when we started shooting in mid-June 2010. As each new script came in for season one, he was still alive, still fighting for what was right and good. I couldn't say by then I knew him very well, but it was obvious T-Dog was a better man than I had originally given him credit for. I owed him every ounce of energy I could give.

From the sun-baked rooftop, closed-down department store, and alleyways of downtown Atlanta to a makeshift camp in an abandoned quarry on the city's outskirts, the cast and crew of the show were confident we were putting together a great body of work. As actors, and characters, we examined themes of great import, analyzing how we viewed ourselves as individuals, communities, and as a vital part of the human family. Politics. Philosophy. Racism. Socialization. We covered it all while kicking zombie butt.

Greg Nicotero and his special effects team created a crop of zombies so gruesome, gooey, and squishy it was easy to get lost in the make believe world. I came out swinging a baseball bat, charging down a zombie in my very first scene on the show. As far as I was concerned, the former human *was* out to eat my brains.

The atmosphere the night we shot the walker attack on the survivors' camp couldn't have been tenser. During the scene, we were set to lose our first major cast member. The impending loss weighed heavily on everyone. In the show, the characters had developed bonds with one another, based on the scripts. Those bonds led them to fight to protect one another without question or hesitation. As actors we felt the same way. Waiting in the dark to run into the camp with Andrew Lincoln, Steven Yeun, and Norman Reedus, I had no doubt the men standing by my side would do the same were the danger real.

Our cast mates in the camp were divided into two groups on top of a hill with the road snaking between them. A silent group of oozing zombies shambled up the road, closing in on their position. Screams rang out over the quarry, filling the night sky with a symphony of human agony. I clutched my rifle, fell into step behind Andrew, Steven, and Norman, and we sprinted through the trees into battle.

I had never been on a set quite like it, where the professional responsibilities mingled seamlessly into interpersonal relationships. Day in and day out we were working our craft, sweating in the hot sun. We hugged, danced, joked, and helped support each other through the physical demands of production. We collectively battled the stifling heat of a humid Georgia summer. The weather became our common adversary, a uniting factor facilitating a rapid embrace of genuinely close relationships. By the time we headed to the Cobb Energy Performing Arts Centre serving as the Centers for Disease Control in the final two episodes of season one, we really were a family—a band of survivors who'd run the gauntlet together and came out stronger for it.

In many ways the actors were quite like the characters they portrayed. Jeffrey DeMunn quickly became the cast's elder statesman, ever ready with words of comfort or wisdom. He had a quick wit and an eagle-eye, noticing every detail. And he didn't shy away from letting you know it. The long days of shooting at our version of the CDC left me exhausted. When I spotted an open chair, I bee-lined for the only available respite I could find. Unbeknownst to me at the time, Jeffrey had been thinking it might be a smart move to find a chair before we launched into the next long scene we were scheduled to shoot. He lovingly skewered me for my occupation of the chair, despite the fact there were women, children, and elders present who could also use a rest. It became a running joke between us. To this day anytime I'm in a room with an open chair and Jeffrey, I make sure to take a chair first, just to see him smile.

Sarah Wayne Callies emerged as our matriarch, stepping in to help organize things like the "Death Dinners" when a cast mate was killed off. It was Sarah, amidst the interminable heat, who proclaimed, "We *are* The Walking Dead" and gave our family form.

Andrew Lincoln led us by example, diving in to each scene with total emotional abandon and professional precision, no matter how hot or tired he was on any given day. Norman Reedus was a somewhat quiet, brooding type. When he did choose to speak, he was likely to toss out a verbal zinger bad enough to make you blush or giggle, or both. Steven Yeun was lively and engaging, a seemingly endless fount of energy.

When production wrapped and we said our goodbyes as season one filming came to a close, none of us knew what the future held. As confident as we were in what we'd performed, we didn't know how well the show would be received. Those of us who survived the explosive finale didn't know if we would make it back should there be a second season. It would be easy for the writers to simply put in a brief eulogy for a character infected, mauled, or otherwise rendered dead in the off-season.

The Walking Dead premiered in October 2010 to strong numbers. Over five million people tuned in. When the final episode for the season aired in early December, the viewers climbed to over six million and the show received broad public and critical acclaim. The masses determined our fate and pre-production was already underway for season two.

Chapter 30
Dead to Rights

It felt like some sort of warped déjà vu, like a nightmare you know you've had before. But as the zombies shuffled down Highway 20 in my direction, I felt something in addition to the terror making my feet twitch with the urge to run. I was home. Reunited with my second family. And there was joy all around us.

Norman and I—and a host of brave zombie extras—shot the scene at least a half-dozen times before it was decided the entire environment for the shot had to be reset. The cars needed to be closer together, Darabont insisted, the pathways more limited. The area where T-Dog lay awaiting certain death in the season two premiere episode would have to be far more claustrophobic for the scene to ring true.

Production outfitted me with a piece of prosthetic skin on my arm. It had a tube underneath running up my arm to my shoulder, down the back of my shirt, and out to the Emmy Award-winning special effects gurus, led by Greg Nicotero and Andy Schoneberg, waiting behind the cars. They gave me a sponge to hold in my other hand filled with red liquid of some sort, so when I cut my arm in the scene, I could slap my other hand on it for an immediate bloody effect until the pumping blood kicked in.

In the highway sequence, T-Dog is one of the last among the survivor's group to spot the herd of zombies approaching. In his haste to find a hiding spot, he slices his arm on a car door and beats a hasty, panicked retreat. T-Dog leaves behind a trail of blood and it becomes obvious when he staggers and bounces off cars, he is unlikely to make it on his own. He falls to the ground with no weapon to defend himself just before a lone zombie comes around a car. T-Dog is saved when Norman Reedus' character, Daryl Dixon, sneaks up behind to stick an arrow in the zombie's brain. As T-Dog begins to waver in and out of consciousness, Daryl drags him to clear ground and tosses the bodies of zombies on top of them both to evade the notice of the passing horde.

We filmed the scene from the time T-Dog spotted the zombies straight through to when Daryl tossed the felled walker on top of him to save his life as one shot, even though the edited version when the episode aired was interspersed with other on-screen action. Getting it right meant doing it as many times as necessary. There was no half stepping. We ran through the scene under the Georgia sun, to the point I thought I would collapse from heat exposure and exertion.

I lurched over to sit on the road's shoulder next to a car, a little wobble-legged from running in the heat. I couldn't help but giggle, thinking I was feeling about as beat as my character. I could've sworn we'd done the scene about five hundred times, though it was probably closer to ten.

Darabont came over and sat next to me on the ground. He placed his arm around my shoulder. "That was awesome work, man." That was one of the things I loved about Frank. He wasn't on the set much by then, but when he was, he was endlessly supportive of the work we did. He stayed with you every step of the way.

We sat there—me covered in bloody grime, he in one of his trademark Hawaiian shirts—in the hot sun for about thirty minutes talking about our lives and where we'd come from. Frank was from Hungary, born in a refugee camp after his parents fled their native country during the 1956 revolution. The family ended up in Chicago before moving on to Los Angeles. Even though he was now an Academy Award-nominated director, Frank was no stranger to want and struggle. We may have come from different backgrounds, but we shared common threads and spoke a familiar language.

Out of the corner of my eye, I saw movement and turned to watch a zombie wiping goop off its face with a napkin. *The Walking Dead* was back. T-Dog would live to fight another day.

* * * * * * * * *

The first indication I had that anything was amiss came when rumors of Frank Darabont's departure from the show exploded across the Internet, infecting social media sites like a zombie plague. The mainstream press picked up the story and questions swarmed in to the cast and crew, asking about the validity of the street talk.

When an email came from one of our producers, Frank's assistant Denise, confirming a departure discussion was underway, I sent Frank a text to express my shock at the news and offering him moral support. Communications flew back and forth. Cast and crewmembers struggled to understand what the blowup meant. On set, small groups of people came together to express their sadness and anger to one another, in an attempt to understand how we were supposed to respond. There were differing opinions emerging, but one thing was clear—no one involved in the show was untouched by Frank's battle amid budget cuts and suggestions for changes to maintain the creative vision and direction he'd set for the project. At one point there seemed to be a growing consensus for the idea of all of us walking off the production set. It affected us all. We believed in him and were grateful for his leadership. He was more than just a director we'd worked with one time. Frank was family like Jon, Sarah, Laurie, and the rest of the show's cast and crew. We broke bread together, sweated in the heat, joked and cringed in appreciation of the horrific beauty being crafted by the special effects department. His departure was a confusing and explosive turn of events.

Frank's response both stunned me and flooded my heart with love. He urged me to stay the course, to keep T-Dog alive as long as *The Walking Dead* universe would allow. I figured other cast members were receiving similar messages.

When the time came for an official discussion about what happened, the room at Raleigh Studios practically rippled with the force of poorly contained emotions. AMC executives, President Charlie Collier and Vice-President Joel Stillerman, flew through the emotional storm in an effort to clear the air. I was seated between Laurie and Jeffrey—two longtime Darabont friends—when the suits promised us the show we all loved and invested so much of ourselves in would continue to be the groundbreaking production we started. Glen Mazzara, who had been an integral part of Frank's production team from early on, would be taking over as showrunner. The only one leaving would be Frank; the rest of the cast and crew would remain. It was a heated meeting. Several cast members chose to make their frustrations with the situation clear in front of everyone. There were a few tears, but most of us said everything we had to say to one another before this meeting was even called. Many of us still did not have a perfectly clear picture why this change was occurring, and the meeting wasn't about explanations. The focus was clearly intended to be on where the show was going in the future.

There wasn't a single person in the room who wanted *The Walking Dead* to end. It was the one thing everybody agreed on. While there was no way the absence of Darabont would not ultimately change the show in myriad ways or alter the departure timelines for some characters, we all placed our faith in what our hearts told us—the show must go on.

* * * * * * * * *

I knew who was speaking before he even finished getting his digs in. "Can I get you something? Maybe a snack? I see you've already got a seat." I shook my head and smiled, looking up at the man who, in a perfect world, would have been the person I called father. He was kind and wise. Anytime I had a call sheet that also had his name on it, I looked forward to work a bit more than usual.

Jeffrey had been on me a lot lately—ever since we returned to film season two and he saw my new Jaguar. I deserved it. When we were approaching the end of season one, I began to consider buying a new vehicle. It felt right to turn to Jeffrey and seek out some advice. In those few summer months we spent together in 2010, Jeffrey became someone whose opinion I not only trusted, but valued. When I told him of my plans, he recommended I consider something a bit more practical, like a Honda; something fuel-efficient with a reputation for needing few repairs. The first thing he asked me when we returned for the second season was what kind of car I decided to buy. He didn't say much beyond agreeing the Jaguar was a beauty when he first saw it.

Jeffrey and Jon hatched an ultimately unsuccessful plan to tie a rope with some aluminum cans or pieces of metal onto my back bumper one day before I drove off the studio lot to make it seem like something was drastically wrong with my new mechanical baby. Fortunately for me, the timing on their go signals was off and they never quite got the opportunity to pull off the prank. Not to be thwarted from their goal, they managed to set themselves up to prank me when I came out of my trailer one day. I did a double take when, out of the corner of my eye, I saw my car bouncing with no one around. It took a couple seconds and the sound of giggling for me to realize Jeffrey was kneeling beside the front bumper, shaking the entire vehicle.

Even with his jokes and good-natured ribbing, Jeffrey's generosity of spirit was never far from the surface. Anytime either one of us got the chance, we'd make our way over to each other in hopes of snagging a quick conversation between takes. We'd talk about life, the show, and our careers. Jeffrey had been born in Buffalo, New York and went on to study theatre in England before launching a career taking him from the National Shakespeare Company to television and film projects—a career spanning three decades. When he told stories about his experiences and how they helped mold him, I couldn't help but wish his influence had been present in my life before.

Whenever we got the opportunity for longer talks, the subject of family would almost inevitably come up. Over the course of the last year, we'd managed to spend a lot of time talking about my mother and father, and how the relative absence of both of them as role models during my younger years left me to learn a lot of life's lessons on my own. Even with the love and guidance I'd gotten from Big Larry and Momzie, there had been gaps I struggled to find a way to fill. Jeffrey, who has two adult children of his own, was a voice of experience. He gave me advice about my children and the worries I harbored, fearing they might choose to travel down paths resembling my brother Tracy's more than my own.

We had something special. The kind of understanding which allowed us to begin a conversation on a Tuesday morning and pick it up on Friday night as if no time had passed at all. Every conversation began with a smile and ended with a hug and the desire for more.

When I realized T-Dog's fevered rants and sickness from an

infection caused by the cut from the season premiere would play out with Dale Horvath, the character Jeffrey played with such incredible force, I was ready for whatever the writers had decided for T-Dog's fate.

We got to spend an entire day together during the filming of the second episode—Bloodletting—the two of us performing our craft under the watchful eye of talented director Ernest Dickerson. Dale's fatherly concern for T-Dog's health following the cut to his arm prompts some discussion from my character about his feelings of latent racism; feeling as the lone black man, he is expendable. Dale reminds him the "cowboys" and "redneck" saved his life, and discovers T-Dog has developed a blood infection from the cut.

Dale was right. In the world the survivor group navigates, any "us versus them" mentality about race the Southern characters may have had before the zombie outbreak was long gone. The peril of their daily existence, of their determination to survive, erased most of the divisions normal society perpetuates ... even if a few echoes remain. It stripped them down to the thoughts, actions, and characteristics most likely to help them survive—loyalty, bravery, friendship. It no longer mattered what these various characters would feel about each other in the normal world. If we removed the zombies and the wholesale destruction of society, it is the world I would want to live in; the kind of place where people band together despite their differences to meet challenges and work toward common goals. When we remove the cultural, religious, and political differences impacting our views, we arrive at one plain truth: we are *all* human beings. All of us are here for a purpose and need one another's love and understanding to survive the world we live in. Circumstance forced the show's characters into a refined ideal of reality whether it was a conscious decision or not. While the world outside the show has no flesh-eating ghouls roaming the streets, there are plenty of societal plagues wearing down our collective souls.

By the end of the arm-cutting story arc, T-Dog is saved by a redneck's stash of medicine, the care of an elderly white man, and a young Asian boy—it made absolutely perfect sense to me.

Chapter 31
Undead in All of Us

The horrible beauty of working on the show was, the closer death circled around our characters and the closer we became as people, the less acting we had to do when the cameras started rolling. That's not to say the blood and guts oozing out of the Nicotero team's zombies were suddenly real. The close-knit family atmosphere permeating *The Walking Dead* production made whatever pre-scene preparations we may have normally done as actors almost secondary to the real emotions we felt for one another and the material we were responsible for.

Our experiences filming the first season of the show left us with the feeling we were prepared for whatever physical and emotional commitment the second season would ask of us. While many of us had an idea where we were heading as the survivor group moved to the faux-serenity of the farmhouse location, the arrival of each new script increased a foreboding feeling, we had not even begun to see the worst this grueling post-apocalyptic world would ask of us.

* * * * * * * * *

The sun baked down on my neck without mercy, coating me in a sheen of sweat, soaking through my T-shirt. It was the hottest day of filming yet on season two, and there wasn't even a hint of breeze to provide any relief whatsoever.

Jon, Laurie, Steven, Jeffrey, Sarah, and Lauren—who we'd all taken to calling LC ("Elsie") on account of her initials—were all staring down at the Well Walker created by the Nicotero team from KNB EFX. It was an amazing piece of work—a mix of a man in a blue computer effects suit, dummy parts, and a real person in makeup—all put together to form a bloated mass of innards and slimy ooze so realistic, a brief glance sent my gorge rising. It was so nasty; I didn't want to look at it until we started filming.

After the first couple takes, the ever-jovial director Billy Gerhart commended me on my performance, but suggested I try it without gagging. I looked around at my cast mates with despair. The gagging as I said my lines had not been an acting device I concocted to enhance the reality of the scene. It wasn't T-Dog ... it was IronE. I turned away from the walker in an attempt to control myself and heard Jeffrey, Greg Nicotero, and my other cast mates giggling behind me. After a few seconds, I thought I was on the verge of getting it under control when Norman decided to chime in from the sidelines, reminding me of my breakfast that morning. It was the sausage rolls in particular he'd honed in on.

When we'd eaten our morning meal, Norman said the turkey sausage rolls looked a bit like human feces. It was a consummate Reedus remark. Norman, who is an intense but friendly guy with a ready—if somehow surprisingly disarming—smile, has an uncanny instinctual ability to know what will make someone uncomfortable and then find a way to make his move. He chose that moment on set to ask me if I was about to puke up the poop I'd eaten for breakfast.

I struggled to shut Norman out of my head. Images of ooze around the well walker and poop-shaped-sausage intermingled in my mind's eye. I was too afraid to open my mouth and possibly hurl to give Norman something back for his kind reminder ... which he saw fit to share with everyone else on set as well. But I knew I had to beat the squeamishness, and walked away from the well area. I leaned on the fence and closed my eyes. Focusing on the warmth of the sun hitting my skin helped me drown out the noise from the cast and crew. After several slow deep breaths I was able to turn and head back over to the well.

By the time I bashed the well walker's brains in and said, "Good thing we didn't do anything stupid ... like shoot it," the ground was covered in blood and body parts.

I knew I'd never look at sausage rolls the same way again.

* * * * * * * * *

Everyone gathered on set the day we knew the survivor group would finally find Sophia. Over the course of several episodes, the search for the missing child drove the action of the characters. The production crew and special effects department kept Madison Lintz, the young lady playing Sophia, hidden from us before shooting. Our characters hadn't seen Sophia since her flight from the highway at the beginning of the season. The director and producers wanted us as actors to have no knowledge of exactly what we would witness coming out of the zombie-hostel-slash-barn on the Greene farm. Hershel Greene's belief that zombies were merely sick people and everyone's desperation to cling to the world as they knew it before the zombiepocalypse began, posed a real danger. We knew what was in the script, the grim nature of its contents, but we would have no chance to prepare for how it would look and feel. It was to be a testimony, for our characters, and for us as actors.

Our characters had been betting on snowballs—praying Sophia would be found unharmed, alive. It was a snowball's chance in hell given the realities of the show's universe. What chance would a preteen girl chased into the forest by zombies stand of surviving on her own, even if search parties scoured the woods to find her? But hope was the last thing these characters sacrificed. It was much the same for us as actors. Losing a colleague from the show became a living nightmare for all of us. A death on the show meant the departure of a family member we loved from our daily lives. We dreaded it.

I looked around at my cast mates and waited for the signal to bring a zombified Madison Lintz out of the barn. Bernthal's character, Shane, had had enough. He was done searching for a little girl, of holding on to the veneer of security in the hope everyone would reach a state of "survival readiness" in his or her own time. He'd had enough waiting for the other members of the group to realize the truth of the world they now lived in. The world had changed, to survive meant to fight. He would force his fellow survivors to see it, no matter the cost.

We were standing in a line when Madison emerged. T-Dog had sprinted forward to take a place between Daryl and Shane, after Shane tore open the barn doors and lured the zombies within to come out in search of fresh meat. The three survivors, with Andrea and Glenn, wiped out the zombies as they exited the barn in a shooting spree. The ground was littered with corpses. Behind us, the Greene family and other characters—Lori, Carl, Carol, and Dale—were in position and waiting.

Madison was the last to leave the barn. She wore sneakers, a pair of khaki colored pants and a blue shirt with a rainbow on it. The kind of shirt you'd expect an innocent little girl, just beginning her journey to adulthood, to be wearing. But she wasn't Madison. She wasn't Sophia. She was a ghoul in search of flesh, tripping her way over the dead bodies scattered on the ground, moving steadily toward a group of people with shock etched on their faces. Our shock went beyond the horrific nature of her appearance. As a father and human being, the thought of a child having their future ripped from them by violence was more inspiration than I needed for the scene. Where I'm from, I had seen it all too often.

When the cameras stopped rolling, the scene erupted with cheers and applause. Madison rose from the ground having delivered a performance far beyond what I pictured in my mind. I joined the celebration, wrapping my arms around her in a hug. When I stepped back to make room for others, I was shaking a little and my hands were red with blood.

* * * * * * * * *

We were all alone in the dark, shivering in the cold. We took our marks in the field, ready to race over to Jeffrey's side. There was no need for us to prepare. Whatever skills we possessed as actors were heightened and thrown into automatic by the adrenaline coursing through our veins. The man who urged us to find joy, draw strength from one another—both as himself and the character left in charge of the survivor group's morality on the show—was about to leave us.

Each time the call for action was given, we had to sprint across the dark field to where Dale lay dying as the result of a walker mauling. In the final cut, audiences saw only about ten to fifteen seconds of Dale's wordless plea for help interspersed with images of other characters' reactions. But during shooting his portion of the death scene lasted well over a minute. Over and over again we had to watch Dale suffer his final moments. Over and over again we had to steel ourselves for a blow that went beyond what would play out on screen. Over and over again I had to remind myself to breathe.

We shot the farmhouse scene—where Dale begs the group to fight back against fear, anger, terror, and hopelessness and cling to their collective humanity—a couple days prior. It was an ensemble performance requiring us to swallow our personal feelings about what his final speech meant and channel our energy into supporting a sublime portrayal of man's final stand. It was as emotional as I'd ever gotten on set; I was unable to stop tearing up over the course of the entire day. Around me I saw only long faces. I hardly spoke between takes, retreating into corners to privately lament the fact I wouldn't be seeing this beautiful man anymore. In a few short days, we would be required to do it again—to say goodbye to another beloved cast mate, Jon Bernthal. Just another twist in the cycle of soul-beating violence dominating the show's universe.

Each death had a particular sadness to it. The details and presumed horror of Sophia's death were left to the worst possible scenario viewers' minds could create—the seemingly senseless death of a young girl who had done no wrong, but whose life was cut short by circumstance. The gut-wrenching violence of Dale's death—a man surrounded by his friends, those who had disappointed him but still enjoyed the warmth of his love. And Shane, dying virtually alone at the hands of a boy quickly losing his innocence, accompanied by the man he'd betrayed as a result of his self-serving choices.

In the aftermath of Dale's death, T-Dog, along with Glenn, Andrea, and Shane, heads out to the farm's perimeter and unleash a deadly fury on zombies in the area. There was brutality there, vengeance diametrically opposed to what I, IronE, felt at the time. Where I was sorrowful and searching for ways to channel my emotion into positive energy, T-Dog had given in to fury. I understood the characters' reactions. Heck, I had seen that kind of response in real life, minus the zombies, of course.

It dawned on me—though I supposed I should have seen it sooner—the zombies in the show were merely the result, not the cause, but somehow still reality. Our society as a whole is home to tens of thousands of zombies already—people driven off-course by a diseased combination of circumstance and choice, whose survival hinges on the destruction of themselves and others. Individuals, families, and entire communities trapped in cycles of violence, racing around a virtual track and field stadium with the cheers and jeers of those in the stands raining down from above. Good people. Worthy souls. Tortured by their inability to find a way out. The survivors are only a small percentage; the majority are lost to the zombie virus, condemned to shamble through a life they no longer believe has any meaning. I had known them all my life.

Chapter 32
Surviving the Dead

Things had changed. The time-line on the show jumped forward several months when we returned to filming for season three. Almost the same amount of time had passed in the real world. *The Walking Dead* grew in our absence with the support of a fan base dedicated to our collective survival.

Season two had premiered to seven-point-three million viewers, around a forty percent jump from the premiere episode in our inaugural season. The fiery end of season two had topped a nine million-strong audience. There was little doubt for any of us; the show's fan-base was growing.

On Internet social media networks I did my best to keep up and respond to the expressions of support coming from fans in the U.S., Canada, Brazil, Argentina, the U.K., Japan, Australia, and elsewhere. At conventions and events in New Jersey, Kentucky, Georgia, and Texas, fans by the thousands made their love for T-Dog and the show known. I listened and loved them back. I found myself humbled by the raw emotion these strangers had and the generosity they shared. There were parents who confided one of the few things they could share with their teenagers and not end up in a fight over was time spent watching *The Walking Dead*. Individuals who said the show inspired them to make survival plans for their own families. Young men and women battling the ravages of cancer treatments took the "never give up" journey of T-Dog, Daryl, Glenn, and the others as inspiration to help them in their own battles. The show, it seemed, was not really about zombies at all. It was about survival, the human condition, and the fight to hold on to the things that matter.

As we regrouped to launch production on season three, the status quo on the show had changed as well. The ragtag group of bickering individuals at different stages of acknowledging how far they were prepared to go to do what needed to be done to survive was gone, replaced by a cohesive unit more akin to a military tactical operations squad. Months on the road left them weary, but united—hardened by a constant battle to stay ahead of the zombies and locate a safe place to find a much-needed respite from the onslaught.

* * * * * * * * *

One of us could have spoken up and alerted Norman to the source of his disquiet. But as the time passed and no one volunteered to help, I figured it was payback for the enjoyment he took from his comfort-robbing shenanigans. He was standing by the fireplace, trusty crossbow in his hands, on what must have been the third time he remarked on the strange smell. He scrunched up his nose and flicked his eyes from spot to spot around the room, determined to figure out what was responsible for the pungent odor.

We were in the midst of filming our first battle scene—the opening sequence of season three, setting the tone for what would be a wild and wacky journey of adversity, love, and sacrifice for the show's main survivor group. Andrew, Norman, and I were on tap—as Rick, Daryl, and T-Dog respectively—to clear a house of zombies and make it safe for the rest of the group to enter. The action makes it obvious, it is nothing new to them. In the months that have passed off-screen, the remaining members of the group coalesced around an operational model for success. Upon entering the home, I would dispatch a zombie with a fire poker; Andrew would drop one with a shot from his pistol. After securing the ground floor, Chandler split off in search of any supplies the house might hold, and Norman headed upstairs to ultimately shoot dinner for everyone.

An abundance of garbage, cracked windows, and dust-covered remnants of furniture made the location a perfect spot for filming. The pervasive grime left the production crew with few additions to make in order to render the atmosphere shot-ready and we made our final preparations to shoot the interior scenes.

I cringed the moment the smell hit my nostrils, immediately

scouring the room for the source of what was undoubtedly the scent of feces. Over the course of the next couple hours, cast and crewmembers caught on to the source and kept their distance from the fireplace. But Andrew and Norman had not managed to identify it, and both kept walking back and forth near the fireplace. I wouldn't have gone so far to bet money on it, but it was pretty likely at least one of them even stepped in it. The first couple times Norman remarked on the smell I thought he might be joking. I had to stifle an ill-timed giggle when it became clear by the end of the day the rest of us knew what he had yet to realize—the poop was in the fireplace just a few inches from his boot. And it looked human.

* * * * * * * * *

The opening moments of season three had a familiar feel to them. The weary group of survivors struggled to hold on to hope, searching out their next meal and a place where they could just be and not have to put up a fight every minute of every day in a world gone completely crazy, stuck in a never-ending cycle of violence and death. They still had one another to lean on, but each individual was fighting their own battle, and it was up to each of them to make their peace with the fight and find a way to succeed.

It was a reality of the human condition every person on the planet faces. There might not be flesh-eating ghouls threatening to break through the doors, but every man, woman, and child faces a lifelong series of challenges and choices that help define their ability to survive and thrive. I had found a way, by keeping love in my heart and my faith in God ever in my mind. I evolved from a young man screaming at his reflection in a bathroom mirror unable to meet the challenges of his existence, to a man capable of using love and faith to propel myself—and hopefully others—forward. Like T-Dog, I had the tools and the drive to fight to survive. I had a group of good battle-tested people around me—Commaleta, Big Larry, Momzie, childhood friends, and newer ones. I knew what it meant to make difficult choices and take up the mantle of responsibility for leading a good life. And like T-Dog—who would subsequently head to a nearby prison for safety—I would fight to the very end to do what was right. I was a survivor.

Chapter 33
Saying Goodbye

I had few words, but an overabundance of love in my heart as cast and crewmates gathered for my final day on the set of *The Walking Dead*. Looking around, I saw faces I'd come accustomed to seeing so often. Andrew. Norman. Steven. Scott. And all the others. Even though I'd known for some time the day was coming and how it might feel, I was overwhelmed by a whirlwind of emotion each time I took my mark for the martini shot—the last scene of the day. As they had done for actors whose characters passed before, even those who weren't involved in filming that day showed up on set to help carry me through. That was the magic of *The Walking Dead*. The magic worth fighting for.

It had been a couple of months since I got the news. Showrunner Glen Mazzara and I played phone tag for well over a week in the late spring of 2012. When we finally connected, he delivered the blow. After three years—gallons of blood, sweat, tears, and enough love to last a lifetime—it was time to let T-Dog go. I didn't know it then, but would learn as the scripts came in over the summer, Mazzara and other executives Denise Huth and Tom Luse, fought alongside the writers to make T-Dog's final moments not only a testament to the character developed on the show, but also the man who portrayed him. T-Dog's faith in his final moments would mirror what the production team knew of my worldview, reflect my determination to remain positive and make decisions from my heart no matter the personal cost.

The sequence of events culminating in the death of not only T-Dog, but also Sarah's character Lori Grimes, was as heart pounding to watch months later on television as it was to film over the course of those final days.

In the episode, the main survivor's group quickly settled in and found comfort in the institutional atmosphere of the largely abandoned prison. They encountered a small group of prisoners— one of whom Andrew's character is forced to kill, and another he locks outside with zombies following an altercation. The second prisoner subsequently opens a gate, allowing zombies to enter portions of the prison the main group worked to make safe.

T-Dog is working with Carol, Melissa McBride's character, to move vehicles out of the prison yard. Rick (Andrew), Daryl (Norman) and Glenn (Steven) are out at the prison perimeter fixing fences and checking overall security. T-Dog and Carol pause to watch the remaining survivors come out of the prison into the sun, leading Scott Wilson's character Hershel Greene, who is recovering from a below-the-knee amputation of his right leg. When all hell breaks loose, the various groups begin a chaotic scramble for safety. At that point T-Dog realizes the gate is open and charges over to close it before more of the shuffling ghouls get through.

That decision—undoubtedly the right one and the kind I hope I'd have the courage to make to save those I love—costs T-Dog his life. In his haste to lock the gate, T-Dog does not notice the zombie shambling up behind him until it sinks its teeth in his neck and rips away a large chunk of skin. But he is not ready to give up. Blood flowing freely from the wound, T-Dog grabs Carol and vows to get her to safety. His faith in God's plan, a belief he reaffirms out loud to Carol, carries him forward to meet his death—not as the result of the infected bite on his throat, but on his own terms, acting to save another. In the end, T-Dog rushes a group of walkers and is ripped apart to give Carol a chance to escape.

* * * * * * * * *

I told the zombie he had no choice but to jump on my back to take his bite. The actor was a bit shorter than me; in order for me to hit my mark and the effect to work properly, he'd have to put in a little gymnastics effort. Each time we ran the shot, the scream coming out of T-Dog's mouth when he was being bitten was a howl of genuine emotion from a man giving every bit of energy he could muster to the final scene of a project that had earned him so much more spiritually than it ever cost physically. When the cameras were running there was no thought in my mind, I was T-Dog—fighting to do what was right. Fighting to survive. But between takes, IronE was fighting a losing battle against thoughts about the show, my cast mates, the fans, and all the life-affirming experiences I'd gotten from participating in a project that was originally only supposed to last a couple of weeks.

As soon as a second assistant director Vince called, "That's the last one for Saty," my Walking Dead family came forward to embrace me. Saty—short for Satyagraha—was the nickname I'd chosen when production asked us to pick names to help prevent spoilers from seeping out about any of the main characters. Satyagraha means nonviolent struggle through truth and love. A practice Dr. Martin Luther King Jr. adopted from Gandhi and used during the American Civil Rights movement. Sarah's nickname was Blue. One by one they said their goodbyes. Cast mates. Executives. Writers. Special effects creators. Camera and sound guys. Extras. Even the transportation director. Each hug carried the weight of true love and raised tears in my eyes.

I struggled to keep my voice clear and I tried to express what they all meant to me. "You've been my family for the last three years and I love each and every one of you with all my heart. It's been an incredible ride, in more ways than I could have imagined. Thank you." I was immensely grateful they didn't need me to say much more than that.

I'd prepared a surprise parting gift for everyone to receive after I was gone. I hoped it would better articulate what I couldn't find the words to express in person. It was a black-and-white marbled plaque with an image of an eagle soaring over the Atlanta skyline on top and a poem in the middle. It read:

> *When destiny beckons*
> *And fate decides the end is near*
> *There is always an undeniable voice within*
> *Whispering words of comfort and confirmation that*
> *Death is only the beginning.*

They all prepared a surprise for me as well—the riot shield T-Dog picked up in the prison and used to fight off zombies. It had been signed by my second family, a token of their respect and love; a physical representation of the emotional bond we have as a family of survivors. In a gesture that left me shaking with raw emotions Norman Reedus—who as a character saved T-Dog's life more than once, and as a man had shown me love and friendship I would carry forth in my heart—walked up and presented the shield. I was so overwhelmed by their love; I couldn't hold it steady.

I looked around at my cast mates, many of them teary-eyed, and was grateful to God for placing *The Walking Dead* in my path, for giving me the opportunity to be part of a family stretching beyond the cast and crew to fans all across the world. So many kind spirits, kindred spirits united in the determination to create something special. I was blessed. To be part of something forcing people to reexamine their beliefs about humanity and sacrifice, and what is worth giving up or holding on to in the fight to survive—a pop-culture phenomenon that resonated across cultural, linguistic, racial, and political barriers. It was exactly where I had hoped to be all those years ago when I promised my younger self in the dingy bathroom mirror I was going to be somebody. I would make a difference.

From doing my best to listen and obey, to speaking to kids and adults alike at different events about the importance of being a cheerful giver, and on to establishing my own place of refuge at the IronE School of the Arts for underprivileged kids, I vowed to continue making a difference. Our true purpose is to help others search for theirs, and on the journey we will find ours. Just as God was continuing to bless me, I would strive to serve as a blessing to others through truth and love. In the bloody, violent world of *The Walking Dead* I found, and still continue to find, all the beauty of the human spirit … I found truth and love.

* * * * * * * * *

Watching myself die on television was like nothing I had ever experienced before. From across the globe came an outpouring of love that positively floored me. The flood of love was so overwhelming and humbling, I thought my chest would burst from it. It was such an emotional evening. I barely held it together for my scheduled appearance on *The Talking Dead* that night. I might have made it if the other guest, none other than the wonderful Gale Anne Hurd, had not spoken so eloquently about my time on the show and the sense of spirituality I brought to the set. She brought me to tears.

Nor would it be the last time T-Dog's battle to survive would leave me virtually speechless. A few weeks after T-Dog's final episode aired I had the opportunity to visit a seventeen-year old, Ernest, who was fighting against an inoperable brain tumor. I saw firsthand what a profound impact the show has had on his life. His eyes were larger than life and he was overwhelmed with excitement to see me—the guy who played his favorite character on his favorite show—when I walked into his hospital room.

Not being able to move anything other than his head—he's a quadriplegic and barely able to speak—I placed my ear in whispering distance of his mouth. He croaked out his sorrow. "Why did you die? You should have stayed alive." Having only weeks to live, Ernest's concern was about a fictional character's survival, and how T-Dog had fought to the very end. T-Dog was his hero.

Little did he know he, Ernest, was IronE's hero. He and all the other individuals out there under such extremely tragic and dire circumstances who manage to stay cheerful and upbeat because they truly appreciate life for what it is—a blessing. They understand, better than most, you have to fight day in and day out to hold on to it—to be a warrior for truth and love. To survive.

Chapter 34
Moving Forward

I looked down at a face so closely resembling my own and smiled. "Come with me E, I've got something I'd like to show you."

I turned and walked down the hallway from his room to ours confident my son would follow. After a few seconds I heard the sound of his footsteps falling on the carpet behind me. I strode directly over to our bed and turned to sit, my hand patting the bed beside me to indicate he should do the same. Ethereal had finally reached the age where he was ready for me to pass on to him one of the most valuable life lessons I'd ever learned.

Prayer has always been a fixture in our family, and God a part of the daily conversation. From my earliest memory, faith in and obedience to God has always been the constant. Every member of my family—Momzie, Grandpa Ray, Commaleta, Big Larry, his sons, Brenda, Tracy—whatever their choices or individual life circumstances, God was ever-present in their hearts.

It's an approach to earthly existence reaching beyond attending mass on Sunday morning. A way of thinking and being, encouraging an open mind and an open heart, and a concentrated effort to make decisions to nurture the soul, no matter how many times you slip. Both our daughters had heard this from me before—timed, Commaleta and I hoped, to a point in their development where they might not completely understand the lesson, but would remember as they grew older.

Ethereal watched quietly as I removed my shoes and socks, and slid off the bed to get down on my knees. With a nod I gestured to him to do the same. He wasn't wearing any shoes or socks, but I told him shoes and socks should always be removed so he'd get it right. Together we clasped our hands before us and I began to recite the Lord's Prayer. I ran Ethereal through the lines, with him repeating after me, twice before I stepped back figuratively, still kneeling next to him, and let him try it on his own.

As he worked his way through the prayer, I couldn't help but think of how many things had changed, and how much remained the same, since I knelt with my uncle and learned the very same thing. Momma Cat was long gone, unable to share the bounty of a good life with her children and grandchildren. Tracy was still in and out of trouble, resigned to living a life full of choices I understood, but could never really accept. I had a loving wife, three beautiful children, supportive friends and family members, and a career which sometimes felt like a dream. Big Larry told me life has to be God first, family second, and everything else would fall into place.

I watched Ethereal stumble a bit through the last couple lines. He worked to remember the order of the words, his brow creased in frustration. After a few seconds, he successfully recited the final line. I reached over to pat my son on the head before wrapping him in a big hug. And I knew—Big Larry had been right.

Acknowledgements

Juliette Terzieff, my friend and colleague, you are the catalyst behind this endeavor. I thank you for not hesitating to come on board when I extended the offer to you to be my co-writer. As I told you at the onset of this project, I feel GOD aligned the stars to bring together kindred spirits to create something beautiful to inspire all of humanity. This book is the culmination of that alignment. Your imprint on this book is invaluable. Your vision, imagination, experiences, insight and voice, not just as a writer but as a human being, were the perfect combination needed to speak to the conscience of humanity. You are the reason this book is worth reading, and I am eternally grateful for your contribution.

LK Gardner-Griffie and R.C. Murphy, your expertise is the exact touch needed to garner respect and give this book life.

I would like to thank the Singleton family for the special combination of blood and genetics which contributes to who I am and makes me proud to be a Singleton.

Thanks to my *The Walking Dead* family for giving me the best all-around experience of my career on the most popular television show in basic cable history and one I will cherish for a lifetime. I would like to thank my *The Blind Side* friends and colleagues for involving me in a project which gave Hollywood the opportunity to recognize my talent. *The Blind Side* inspired so many people around the world and reminded us there are good people who, unconditionally, do good things in the world. I would like to thank The Houghton Talent Agency in Atlanta, GA for representing me when no other agency would.

To my family, friends, teachers, mentors, and fans, I am deeply indebted to you for your undying love and support. Ethelrine Singleton, Larry Singleton, Edward Bozeman, Jasper Watts, Michael Rooker and Jeffrey DeMunn, your contributions to this effort are greatly appreciated.

Of course, none of this would be possible without GOD who gave me an extra boost of motivation, inspiration, loyalty, devotion, love, and more, through the person without whom this book would not be possible ... my wife, Commaleta. You are the most talented and beautiful human being on planet Earth. Your spirit transcends the human experience. No human being is perfect, but you are extremely close. You complete me. Thank you Heavven, Nevvaeh and Ethereal for being the best kids parents could have.

To all of humanity—Truth & Love!

Where to find out more about IronE Singleton:

Website:
http://www.ironesingleton.com/

Twitter:
http://twitter.com/IronESingleton

Facebook:
https://www.facebook.com/pages/IronE-Singleton/116408841720422

IMDB:
http://www.imdb.com/name/nm1533036/

General information or enquires:
booking@ironesingleton.com

Juliette Terzieff is a former foreign war correspondent with combat training, human rights journalist, fiction and non-fiction writer, and public speaker. She has worked and lived in various locations around the world including war zones in the Balkans, South Asia, and the Middle East. Her work has appeared in international print and media outlets such as CNN, Newsweek and the San Francisco Chronicle. She has covered complex political, globalization, and human rights issues from human trafficking and child labor to American politics and international relations.

Juliette writes and edits newsletters for SmartBrief on development, humanitarian aid, public health concerns, veterans' issues, and international policy, and serves as co-founder and commander-in-chief of the Zombie Survival Crew. She also works in celebrity event management with dozens of actors, writers and musicians. During the writing of this book, Juliette expressed how blessed and fortunate she is to have the opportunity to know such talented and inspiring individuals as Robert 'IronE' Singleton.

Where to find out more about Juliette Terzieff:

Website:
http://www.julietteterzieff.com/

Twitter:
http://twitter.com/jterzieff

Facebook:
http://www.facebook.com/JulietteTerzieff